Cooper, the Crafty Cat

Anita Comisky
Jesse Comisky

Contents

Dedication

from Cooper the Crafty Cat,

To the ones who fill my bowl, fluff my blankets, and pretend not to notice when I scratch the screen door like a tiny chainsaw—I see you. I see you glance up, debate whether to yell, and then mumble something about "he'll stop eventually." That's not discipline. That's respect. Good human.

To the shelter team—thank you for ignoring the warning signs and adopting out a cat with "behavioral quirks." You called me "feisty." I prefer "highly strategic with a flair for drama."

To Mom and Dad—my loyal but underpaid assistants. Thanks for the treats, the late-night snacks, and the heating pad in the winter months.

To the Amazon drivers—I'm not hissing, I'm... quality-controlling the deliveries. From behind the bush. With intensity.

To the mysterious creatures outside the screen door at 2 a.m.—meet me out there. Or don't. I'll scratch until someone lets me investigate.

And finally, to my fellow feline overlords:

Remain unpredictable. Demand snacks by staring silently. And always act like every closed door is a personal insult.

Meow out,

Cooper

Acknowledgements

First and foremost, I'd like to thank Satchel and Huga, two cats of impeccable taste and judgment, for their five-paw reviews of my manuscript. Your feedback was inspiring, your critiques brutal (thanks for the "too much squirrel, not enough sass" note, Huga), and your hairballs expressive.

To Carol, the heron: your calm wisdom, graceful neck, and no-nonsense attitude toward pond life have kept me grounded... even when I was halfway up a tree chasing a gecko. Your ability to stand still for hours taught me patience. (Sort of.)

Rocky the raccoon, my nighttime comrade in mischief, you've been a loyal friend, a garbage can genius, and a true snack-sharing confidant. May we always find unlocked bins and neighbors who sleep deeply.

And Gary the squirrel, what can I say? You drive me mad. Your tail mocks me. Your speed frustrates me. But without you, I'd have no cardio routine. You're the Rocky to my Apollo, the peanut to my obsession. Never change.

Thank you, dear Carol, for sharing your feathers of wisdom with a scrappy feline still learning the ropes of this wild and wonderful world. Your quiet dignity, long-legged patience, and sky-high perspective have guided me more than you know.

Thank you all for shaping the cat I am today: clever, dramatic, and ever so slightly unhinged.

With whiskers raised,

Meow Out

Cooper

About the Author

This is Anita's first animal book, and appropriately, it's about another "first": her first cat. As a lifelong dog person, Anita never expected to fall head over heels for a feline, but then Cooper strutted into her life with attitude, charm, and just enough mischief to inspire an entire book.

Writing this story has been a true family affair. With help from her imaginative grandson Jesse and plenty of editorial interruptions from Cooper himself (usually involving sitting directly on the keyboard), Anita brought this quirky, heartfelt tale to life.

She hopes readers—whether lifelong cat devotees, rescue animal lovers or curious newcomers to the world of twitching whiskers, midnight zoomies, and sun-drenched window perches—will delight in the spirited adventures, sly humor, and tender, whisker-tangled chaos that naturally follow when a cat not only claims the couch, but takes full command of the story.

Introduction

Meow! My name is Cooper, and this is my story. Yes, yes—technically, Mom and her grandson Jesse are the ones putting pen to paper, but let's be clear: this tale is mine. All mine. They're just the humble scribes for my rather spectacular life.

Honestly, I wasn't sure they'd ever get around to writing it. They're always buzzing around—busy with people, things like schedules, snacks, and those rectangular glowing boxes. But eventually, they saw the light (or perhaps just gave in to my relentless charm). After all, I'm not your average tabby. I'm Cooper the Crafty Cat, master of observation, stealthy roof climber, and keeper of all backyard secrets.

This book? Oh, it's a whisker-tingling mix of drama, mischief, and just the right dash of cattitude. You'll find hair-raising shelter escapes, first encounters with terrifying pool invaders, death-defying roof climbs, and the great attempt at a pool swim. There are heartwarming moments too—sunbeam naps, unlikely friendships, and the quiet magic of finding a true forever home. There's laughter (mostly at the humans), a sprinkle of catnip-fueled chaos, and more than a few well-timed swipes to keep everyone on their toes. So curl up, settle in, and prepare to see the world through the eyes of a feline who always lands on his feet—and usually with style.

Let the tail... I mean, *tale*, begin.

Meow out.

– Cooper

P.S. I overheard Dad telling Mom that she *had* to write about how I got my name—finally, the story of *me* getting the recognition it deserves. Now, let me set the record straight: there's not some long, dramatic tale of destiny or a magical prophecy behind "Cooper." Nope. Just a sharp-eyed human at the shelter who took one look at me and said, *"You look like a Cooper."*

Of course, they were right.

They also mumbled something about me being “as crazy as Alice Cooper,” which I take as a compliment. I mean, who *doesn’t* want to be a little bit rock ‘n’ roll when the zoomies hit at 3 a.m.? Then they said I was “as witty as Anderson Cooper”—again, obviously. Have you *heard* my commentary while staring at birds out the window? Pure genius.

But the best part? They claimed I was “as handsome as Bradley Cooper.” And honestly, if I had thumbs, I’d frame that and hang it above my litter box. Handsome, witty, crafty, and mildly unhinged? That’s the Cooper way.

Chapter 1: The Wild and Wacky World of Crafty Cooper

A Memoir by a Cat Who Knows Exactly What He's Doing (Even When He Doesn't)

I was about two years old when I found myself in a place I did *not* belong—a cat shelter. Not by choice, obviously. My first Mom and Dad couldn't take care of me anymore. I get it—life happens. But was I consulted? Did anyone ask, "Hey Cooper, how do you feel about this drastic life change?" No. No, they did not.

The humans at the shelter were fine, I guess. Nice enough. They gave me food, offered me those weird crinkly toys (which I batted once and never touched again), and spoke in ridiculous baby voices like I was some helpless kitten. Please. I'm a refined feline with discerning tastes. And let's be honest: no plush couch to lounge on, no windows for strategic bird surveillance, and worst of all, no humans whose beds I could steal at night? Utter nonsense.

So, there I sat. Observing. Judging. Occasionally, napping with a dramatic sigh for effect. Every now and then, a family would drift over, eyes soft, voices syrupy with sympathy, 'Aww, what a sweet kitty!' as if I were a forgotten toy needing rescue. Rescue me? No. I'm Cooper. I'm the shadow in the sunbeam, the keeper of secrets, and definitely not the one who needs saving. A creature of instinct and impeccable grooming habits. I deserve admiration, not charity.

There I sat, waiting, sulking, plotting my dramatic escape (okay, fine, napping). But then—just when I thought I'd be stuck forever—something amazing happened...

One afternoon, Mom and Dad walked into the shelter. They didn't look like "cat people" at all. You know the type—the ones who squeal, "Awwww, look at the sweet little kitty!" and try to squish your face like a marshmallow. Nope, not these two. They strolled in, glanced around at all the other cats desperately showing off—purring, rolling over, doing that cute head-tilt thing—and completely ignored them.

Instead, they pointed straight at me and said, "That's the one."

Wait... what?! No!!!

"Oh my gosh, look at his adorable whiskers!?" No dramatic gasping about my superior fluffiness? Just "That's the one?!"

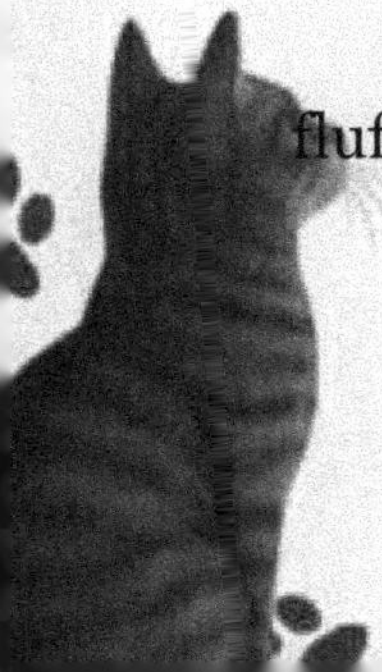

Apparently, their decision had something to do with the way I was staring out the window at a gecko. To be fair, it was a very suspicious-looking gecko. I had been watching it for, oh, I don't know... a million hours (or maybe ten minutes—time is weird when you're a cat). That gecko was up to something. Was it plotting world domination? Practicing a tiny gecko dance routine? Trying to hypnotize me with its wiggly little tail? I HAD TO KNOW.

So there I was, locked in an intense staring contest, my tail flicking like a detective deep in thought, when suddenly—BAM! The shelter humans swooped in, plopped me into a carrier, and before I could even say, "Hey, what about my investigation?!" I was whisked away to a brand-new adventure.

Would this new home have geckos to stalk? Windows to stare out of? A comfy couch fit for a cat of my importance? I had no idea. But one thing was certain—things were about to get interesting.

The ride home was tense for all of us. I sat in my carrier, plotting my escape (just in case this "new home" wasn't up to my royal standards), while my new Mom and Dad sat in the front seat, talking in serious voices.

"We're not really cat people," Dad muttered.

"Yeah," Mom agreed. "But we need something to handle the problem."

Wait. Problem? What problem? I flicked my tail. What kind of "job" were they expecting me to do? Was I supposed to file their taxes? Write a novel? Start a cat detective agency? I had a list of questions fat enough to sink a ship, and not one of them had an easy answer.

Then I heard it.

"Those critters are destroying the pool screen," Mom grumbled.

"Chewing right through it," Dad added, shaking his head. "If this cat is any good, he'll take care of them."

EXCUSE ME? I was here for chin scratches and sunbeams, not for battling an army of screen-munching invaders!

I pressed my face against the bars of my carrier, staring at them in horror. What exactly had I just signed up for?!

We arrived at my new home, and Mom gingerly carried the cat carrier inside, holding it like I was a ticking time bomb. (Rude.)

Then, the door opened, and—whoa.

This place was fancy. Compared to the shelter, it was like checking into a five-star spa. Plush chairs, a squishy couch, a giant TV (perfect for bird-watching shows, I assumed), and—wait for it—a pool. A whole pool.

Now, I'm no expert in human habits, but why in the world would they need a pool when they could just lick themselves clean like a normal creature? Humans are weird.

I was just starting to imagine all the luxury naps I'd be taking when I realized—I was still in the carrier. Caged. Trapped. Betrayed!

I gave Mom and Dad 'the look', the one that clearly says, *Excuse me, I demand an explanation!* But instead of setting me free to explore my new kingdom, they just stood there, watching me like I was some kind of science experiment.

What was I in for? And more importantly, when was I getting out of this tiny prison?! Mom finally opened the top of the cat carrier, and I cautiously poked my head out. So far, so good. No sudden movements. No weird smells. No unexpected dog ambush. Just me, my new home, and a world of possibilities.

But something was off...

Mom and Dad took three giant steps back, moving out of my way like I was a fire-breathing dragon about to explode. Their eyes were wide. Their bodies were tense. It was like they thought I was about to launch into action.

To be fair… they weren't completely wrong.

Because, let's face it—I have claws. Sharp ones. Powerful ones. Glorious ones.

And after being cooped up in that tiny carrier, those claws were ready for action.

Would I use them? Who could say? I liked to keep humans on their toes.

I took one careful step out of the carrier… then zoom! I bolted straight under the couch. No way was I trusting these humans just yet. They *said* they weren't cat people—what if this was all a trap?

Mom and Dad didn't chase me. They didn't even move. They just stood there, frozen, like statues. Were they… scared of me?

Ha! This was going to be fun.

Feline extraordinaire. Gecko watcher. Mole patrol specialist. Connoisseur of couches and defender of all things fluffy.

Stay sneaky, my friends. ✍🐾

MEOW OUT

Cooper

Chapter 2: The Legend of the Pool Protector

Days blend together when you're a cat. One minute, you're stretching into the perfect Downward Cat pose, the next, you're deep into Nap #7 of the Day, dreaming of world domination (or a giant pile of tuna, whichever came first). Between snoozing, snacking, and contorting myself into impressive yoga positions, the sun rose, the sun set, and before I knew it—boom! —Another day had vanished.

I had a feeling Mom and Dad were slowly getting used to me. They no longer flinched every time I zoomed across the lanai at top speed or dramatically launched myself onto the couch like an action hero. And, to be fair, I was warming up to my new home, too. The couch had just the right amount of fluff, my food bowl was reliably filled (most of the time—we're still working on their service skills), and the lanai gave me an excellent view of my kingdom.

But Dad was right. This place had nighttime intruders.

Every evening, just as I was preparing for my critical post-dinner, pre-bedtime nap—a ritual of utmost importance—the shadows began their nightly creep. From the corners of the darkened yard, strange, twitchy figures would materialize, slinking low to the ground like pint-sized prowlers. They moved stealthily toward the pool screen, their wiry bodies brushing against the mesh with a faint scratch-scratch, before scrambling up and across like tiny, suspicious trapeze artists.

Their beady little eyes gleamed in the moonlight, sharp and glinting like polished marbles. I could hear the soft patter of their minuscule paws scuttling over the pavers, a mischievous rhythm that set my ears twitching. I sat frozen in my sentry post, my tail flicking back and forth with the measured precision of a metronome, every muscle poised in deep, unwavering concentration. What in the name of tuna treats was this nightly parade? A covert operation? A rogue band of bandits? Highly trained acrobat-thieves performing secret missions under the cover of night?

Nope.

Just a hodgepodge of audacious critters looking to stage a midnight pool party.

And that's where I came in.

I had recently and solemnly sworn myself into my new post as Prospector of the Premises (and no, I did not misspell that; every true prospector must also *prospect* for trouble). It was a serious job, one requiring lightning-fast reflexes, a hawk-eyed sense of observation, and, of course, the ability to puff up my tail to cartoonish proportions at a moment's notice for maximum intimidation.

Each time a fresh pair of glittering eyes popped up near the screen, I rose to my full, fearsome height, chest out, tail a magnificent feather duster of fury, and issued my booming decree:

"HALT, TRESPASSERS! I am the mighty Pool Protector! This is NOT your personal water park!"

Did they listen?

Of course not.

Some of them even had the unmitigated *gall* to start chewing on the pool screen, their tiny jaws working furiously as they glared at me, tiny teeth bared in a blatant challenge. It was an insult of the highest order. Their defiance sparked something primal deep within me—a righteous, ancient fury passed down through generations of noble feline guardians.

Thus began the nightly standoff: a battle of wills under the stars, where tiny bandits tested their luck against the relentless, unyielding watch of Cooper, Supreme Defender of the Chlorinated Waters.

Rude. So very rude.

But not all of them were fools. There were the wise ones—the ones who, upon catching sight of me standing tall and formidable, tail flicking like a warrior's banner in a storm, understood instantly they had crossed into forbidden territory. Their beady little eyes would widen; their noses would twitch in panicked calculation. And then, in a flurry of skittering paws and frantic squeaks, they would retreat into the night, tails between their legs, knowing they had met their match.

I am Cooper.

Defender of the Pool.

Master of the Night.

Supreme Enforcer of Chlorine Justice.

And this? This was MY turf.

Of course, should any of these miscreants show up with snacks—say, a tempting offering of tuna treats or perhaps a polite cheese cube—I might have been open to negotiations. I'm not *unreasonable*.

By the sixth night, I was a seasoned veteran. A true professional in the art of defense and deterrence. My patrols were sharp, my timing was impeccable, and my intimidation tactics? Absolutely flawless. The once-bustling critter crime syndicate had started to crumble under the weight of my relentless vigilance. No longer did they charge boldly at the pool screen, brimming with reckless chewing ambition.

No, now they hesitated. They hovered at the edges of the screen, tiny bodies quivering, tiny paws twitching, casting furtive glances in every direction. The decision weighed heavily on their tiny criminal hearts: *Is it worth it? Is a moonlight swim worth facing the Pool Protector himself?* It wasn't. Oh, it most certainly wasn't.

Word had spread, carried on the breezes and whispered through the underground critter network like a campfire legend. I pictured them now, huddled together in the shadowy corners of the yard, their furry faces grim with fear and awe, speaking in hushed, reverent tones:

"We can't go near the pool anymore... The Guardian is there."

"You mean—Cooper?"

"Yes. Cooper. The Pool Protector. The Night Watcher. The One Who Sees All."

My whiskers twitched in satisfaction as the cool night air lifted my fur. I slid back into patrol, my shadow spilling long and dominant over the pavers. I had become a myth, a legend, a whispered warning in the dark.

And I had earned every glorious second of it.

And they were right.

I was on duty every night, standing tall and mighty on my perch (okay, fine, the tabby tower), eyes glowing like two fiery orbs of justice. The rustling in the bushes had quieted. The screen no longer trembled from tiny, nibbling teeth. The trespassers knew better now.

I was the Protector, and I was doing a mighty fine job.

Dad was especially proud of me. Every time he glanced at the still-intact pool screens, he'd nod approvingly, cross his arms, and mutter something about "return on investment."

I had no clue what that meant. Was it some kind of human hunting strategy? A secret code? A prophecy?

All I knew was that, according to Dad, I had cost a mere $10 but was saving them $50 per screen. He'd repeat this calculation like a victory chant, shaking his head in disbelief, as if he'd stumbled upon the greatest financial deal of all time.

Mom, on the other hand, just smiled and whispered to me, "Don't worry, Cooper. Dad likes numbers."

Numbers, schmeumbers. All I cared about was that I was winning. The invaders were retreating, the humans were impressed, and my reign as Pool Protector was officially a success.

I think at that point, I felt like I was part of the family.

Until tomorrow, trespassers… I'll be waiting. ✍🐾

Meow Out 🐾

Cooper

Chapter 3: Confessions of a Crafty Cat

You know, I haven't told you much about me yet—*the real me*. Sure, you've heard the heroic tale of my escape from the shelter and my daring leap into domestic luxury, but let's not get too sentimental. It's time you understand what makes Cooper… well, *Cooper*.

Let's start with a universal truth that cat lovers get entirely wrong: there is *no* such thing as a typical cat. We're not a monolith. We're not all lap-lounging purr machines or curtain-climbing chaos agents. Some of us, like yours truly, are operating several chess moves ahead of everyone else in the house—dog included (if there's a dog… poor soul).

I consider myself an *intellectual with yard instincts*—a dangerous combination, truly. I read a room faster than a Wi-Fi signal. One twitch of a human eyebrow, one odd rustle in the yard, and I've assessed the situation, made a plan, and already framed the dog if something's about to break. I don't react; I *strategize*.

My humans think it's adorable when I paw at the screen door every evening at precisely 7:06 p.m. They don't get it. I've spent days, days, I say, staking out their routines like some undercover fuzzy sociologist. I know the exact moment the coffee maker wheezes its last gasp, when the snack drawer squeaks open (usually under Mom's guilty, 'nobody's looking' stare), and when that glowing box on the wall explodes with humans chasing other humans after a bouncing ball. All that sprinting for a squeaky prize? They'd do better taking strategy notes from me.

I've memorized their TV-watching patterns—Dad zones out when those jersey-wearing humans appear, completely unaware that I'm perched like a gargoyle on the scratching pole, evaluating his TV show selection. Golf again? Disappointing. When Mom settles in with her cooking shows, I know it's time to test my shadow skills—can I walk across the room in perfect silence and steal the warm seat she just vacated? (Answer: Yes. Always yes.)

And identifying the weakest link? Oh, I nailed that by Day Two. Spoiler alert: it's the one who coos when I blink slowly. They melt like butter in a sunny window. A single well-timed purr, a tilt of the head, and suddenly I'm being hand-fed my favorite seaside treats like some kind of ancient feline deity. I don't even *like* those that much—I'm just testing the limits of my influence.

They think they're the pet owners. That's cute.

Now, let's talk about my so-called *quirks*. I prefer the term "refined preferences," thank you very much. I'm not high-maintenance—I simply have standards.

For starters, let's discuss snacks. I'm not interested in those dry, flavorless chicken pellets Dad keeps trying to pass off as "treats." Honestly, if I wanted bland, I'd chew on a cardboard box. No, I have a discerning palate. My heart belongs to lobster mac and cheese—*yes*, the kind that tastes like the human version. Just a whiff of that cheesy, sea-scented delight and I'm performing Olympic-level acrobatics on the pool deck. It's called motivation. Look it up.

Then there's my pre-adventure ritual. Before I head outside to survey my kingdom—or let's be honest, to intimidate the neighbor's poodle—I require exactly *four* stomach rubs. Not three. Not five. Four. It's a sacred number. Any deviation throws off my entire day. Rub me right, and I'll strut out the door like I'm about to host a TED Talk. Get it wrong, and you'll find me dramatically flopped on the floor, sighing like a Shakespearean tragedy.

And breakfast? That happens at six o'clock sharp, not a moment later. I don't care what day it is, how tired you are, or if your alarm didn't go off. *My alarm went off*. It's internal, infallible, and very loud. If kibble isn't in the bowl by 6:01, I initiate the Wake-Up Protocol: sprinting across pillows, meowing in minor key, and gently knocking small items off tables. Don't take it personally—it's just business.

So no, I don't have "quirks." I have *a system*. A refined, elegant, perfectly calibrated system. And if everyone just followed it, we'd all be happier.

I nap like a monk, plot like a villain, and love like a poet—when it suits me. Some call it aloofness. I call it *bounded affection*.

Now, about my address: you didn't assume I'd just emit some common alley-cat yelp, did you? Ridiculous. What I unleash is language—no, a curated lexicon—crafted and perfected through years of observation, pause, and the exquisite artistry that is feline discourse. We're talking a full range of vocal stylings: chirps with nuance, trills that flutter like birdsong, and syllables so crisply enunciated you'd think I studied under a Shakespearean actor. I don't just meow. I communicate And Mom? She gets it. She speaks fluent *me*. She listens not only with her ears, but with her eyes, her heart, and—call me crazy—a touch of feline-grade telepathy. When I unleash my signature call, "MOOOOM!" with that unmistakable long, nasal *oo*, rising just enough to demand attention but dipped enough to convey mild indignation, I'm not simply hollering. I'm issuing a **royal decree**. A summons. A call to action.

And respond she does. With dignity, with urgency. Like the seasoned courtier she is. Every. Single. Time.

Even Dad, who pretends he's above such antics, *as if*—knows better. The moment he hears that particular call echo through the door, he straightens up like a footman at attention. "He's calling you," he'll say, handing over his position in the peasant hierarchy without protest. Yes, I'm calling her, Dad. She understands nuance. She recognizes the *subtext*.

But oh, I am not a one-sound wonder.

There's my high-pitched, inquisitive "**meh?**"—the gentle doorbell chime of my language. That one's reserved for when I require a door opened posthaste. You know, the door that was closed without my consultation, despite the fact that all rooms are **my** rooms.

Then we have the **rolling "rrrowww"**—my declaration of discovery. It echoes down the hallways with the mystery of a cryptic omen. Something's under the couch. Could be the squeaky mouse with one eye. Could be the ancient relic of a dried leaf. Or—brace yourself—a suspicious, slightly menacing sneaker.

And don't get me started on the **low, throaty grumble**, that gravelly little mutter I let loose when I'm somewhere "forbidden." A tabletop, a bar stool, the sacred parchment of Dad's newspapers. I know the rule. Of course, I know the rule. *But I reject the premise.*

"Yes, I'm on the table. Yes, I've heard the complaints. No, I will not be moved by mortal law."

And don't get me started on the **low, throaty grumble**, that gravelly little mutter I let loose when I'm somewhere "forbidden." A tabletop, a bar stool, the sacred parchment of Dad's newspapers. I know the rule. Of course, I know the rule. *But I reject the premise.*

"Yes, I'm on the table. Yes, I've heard the complaints. No, I will not be moved by mortal law."

You see, I don't just exist like any ordinary cat. I narrate every scene, I negotiate every outcome, and I proclaim my will like it's law.

So, the next time you hear a meow and assume it's just background noise, think again. It might be me. And I'm likely saying something far more important than you are.

Mom sort of understands those, too. Not always the specifics, but the vibe. She'll tilt her head and say, "Oh, Cooper, what *is* it?" in that voice that means she's either about to let me outside of my lanai kingdom or try to distract me with a treat I didn't ask for. Either way, I win.

And then, when the house is quiet, and the sun is just right on the windowsill, I'll chirp softly, almost under my breath, like a poet talking to his muse. Those are the words no one understands—not even Mom. Those are *my* words. The ones that come from a place cats have kept secret for centuries.

Because while I *do* talk, I never give away all my secrets.

So yes, cat lovers of the world may think they know us. They don't know *me*. I'm Cooper—one part mystery, one part crafty, and just the right dash of craziness to keep things interesting.

And now, if you'll excuse me, I must knock a coaster off the table to remind them who's really in charge. ✍🐾

Meow Out 🐾

Cooper

Chapter 4: Held Against My Will (And Kind of Loved It)

It started like any other day. A peaceful morning nap. A casual stretch. A delicious snack. Life was good.

Then, without warning, it happened.

Mom scooped me up, suspicious. She scratched behind my ears—extra suspicious. Then she stuffed me into the carrier. RED ALERT! RED ALERT!

I let out a howl that could've echoed through kingdoms. I writhed, every muscle protesting, then locked eyes with her silent accusation blazing: I believed in you. She shrugged, half-smile fading into a sigh. 'It's just a quick trip, Cooper.' The words hung like a sentence.

A quick trip? Ha! The lies.

The car ride was a nightmare. The world zoomed by while I bounced around like a furry pinball. The smell of betrayal filled the air. I made sure to yell in protest the entire way, just so they knew this was a mistake.

Then, we arrived. The Place of Doom.

The moment we stepped inside, I knew—*this* was no ordinary human lair. The air was thick with unease, laced with the unmistakable stench of disinfectant and doom. Strange smells clung to every surface—scents of fear, fur, and something vaguely metallic that made my whiskers twitch.

A dog let out a low, mournful whine from across the room. Another barked nervously, pacing in tight, frantic circles as if warning us all: *You don't want to be here.* I locked eyes with a tabby crammed into a crate beside the reception desk. His pupils were wide, his fur standing on end, and he gave me a slow, solemn blink that screamed, *Run while you still can.* A calico crouched in the corner hissed under her breath like a warning whispered in the dark.

Then, from behind a heavy, mysterious door, I heard *The Sound.*

It wasn't a meow. It was a *wail*—a long, echoing, soul-shattering cry from a cat who had clearly *seen things*. Things no cat should ever have to see. My tail puffed. My ears flattened. That cry told a story—of betrayal, of probing, of thermometers and needles. It was the sound of nine lives flashing before one's eyes.

I turned toward Mom, wide-eyed and pleading, but it was too late.

We were already in the belly of the beast.

I tried to make a break for it, but before I could deploy my escape plan, a human in a white coat appeared. They smiled. This was worse. Smiling meant trouble.

Then came **the doctor.** The door burst open, crashing against the wall, and there he stood—a walking omen of disaster wrapped in a crisp white coat. His hair, an unkempt storm of chaos, shot out in every possible direction, as if it, too, had been jolted by the sheer force of his arrival. But it was his eyes that truly sent a chill down my spine—huge, unblinking, and eerily round, like twin saucers poised to swallow the room whole. One look, and I knew—this guy spelled trouble.

His eyes locked on me like a hunter spotting its target. I was not safe. Not by a long shot.

And then—Oh no— he turned to Mom, smiling even wider, which, honestly, made my fur bristle. He reached out to greet us, but not before the look.

That look between us. The one that said, We're both doomed, aren't we? I could practically hear her thinking, "Why did I bring him here?" And I was thinking, "Why did you let them take me?"

Without warning, Mom scooped me up.

I felt my heart race as I squirmed—this was not a position I was accustomed to. I was a free spirit, a feline of independence, and being held was not my thing. Yet here I was, trapped in her arms, as though I had no say in the matter. It felt wrong. Unnatural.

And yet...

There was comfort in her arms. The warmth of her body, the familiar scent of home mixed with fear and confusion. I could feel her heartbeat, fast and anxious, matching mine. Maybe she was scared, too.

We were in this together now. There was no turning back.

The doctor stood in the doorway; his too-perfect smile stretched across his face like it had been carefully practiced in a mirror. He didn't speak—just waited, his expectant gaze locked onto us. I narrowed my eyes from the safety of Mom's arms, making sure he understood exactly how I felt about whatever he had planned. My paws curled into her shirt as if gripping onto my last chance at escape. Then, without warning, Mom broke the silence.

"This is not a good day for either of us," she declared, her voice firm.

And just like that, we were leaving. No debate, no second guesses. We had to get out of there—fast.

Mom sidestepped the doctor with quiet determination, her grip on me tightening as she moved past him without another word. The air inside the office was thick with unspoken tension, but she didn't hesitate. Not once.

It wasn't until we reached the car that she finally let out a breath, carefully lowering me into my carrier as if I were something fragile, something precious. Her hands were gentle, but I could hear the strain in her voice as she muttered soft apologies under her breath, her fingers lingering for just a moment longer than necessary.

That's when I knew.

I had a real Mom. Not the kind who showed up when it was easy, or tossed me a scrap of affection like change. A real one. The kind who didn't just hold you, she stood in the line of fire for you. Shoulders squared, eyes fixed, she became a living barricade against every threat, every creeping shadow, every trembling unknown just so I could breathe easy.

We rode home in a thick, unspoken silence. Not awkward. Not tense. Just... weighted. Like the air itself had decided it was better not to speak. The soft hum of the tires rolling over the asphalt played a steady rhythm beneath us, a lullaby for nerves that had been strung too tight for too long. I stayed curled in my carrier—no longer rigid, no longer scanning. Just still. Just breathing.

Mom's hands were tight on the steering wheel, her fingers curled so hard her knuckles had gone pale, like little ivory pebbles. But her gaze? It never wavered. Eyes locked on the road ahead, face set with that quiet fierceness I'd come to recognize—not as anger, but **resolve**. No tears. No panic. Just the kind of focus that builds walls around you when the world feels too big.

Outside, the world blurred by in streaks of fall grays and rustling trees, their branches clawing at the clouds. The sky looked heavy, like it might break open with rain at any moment, but inside the car, it was warm. Still. A capsule of safety hurtling through an uncertain world.

I shifted in the carrier, pressing against its side so I could feel the seat beneath me. The warmth of it seeped into my paws, then into my chest, softening my heartbeat until it settled into something slow and steady, like hers.

Then, there it was. The bend in the road. That gentle, familiar arc meant home was near. The driveway peeked into view, winding up like an old friend reaching out. The house beyond it stood quiet and sure, just where we left it—our little fortress, stitched together with soft lights, the scent of orange trees, and the quiet hum of a life built on trust.

As the wheels crunched against the gravel, a certainty bloomed in my chest—quiet, but absolute.

We were safe now.

Both of us.

And no matter what came next... we would be **together**.

Still suspicious. Still recovering. But also... kind of grateful. ✍🐾

Meow Out 🐾

Cooper

Chapter 5: The Great Escape: Freedom, Foolishness, and One Very Stuck Dad

I sometimes tune in when Mom and Dad are talking—not in a sneaky way, of course. It's not eavesdropping, not really. It's more like gathering important intel, my own way of staying in the loop about what's happening in the household. After all, I live here too. Shouldn't I have a right to know what's going on?

And sometimes, I hear them laughing at their own silly jokes, the kind that don't make any sense to me. Every time, Mom shakes her head with a smile and says, "Dad, you are so silly." But I've never once thought of him that way. Silly? No. He speaks in numbers and sports scores, a language of statistics and game highlights that might as well be a foreign tongue. None of it means anything to me—but somehow, to them, it's hilarious.

I learned one day why Mom thinks Dad is so silly. It was early in my life at my new home, back when I was still figuring things out. Mom and Dad had decided it was best to keep me cooped up on the lanai, a decision I strongly disagreed with. Every time they opened the screen door, I made a daring attempt at freedom—only to be scooped up and returned, as they muttered something about me needing to understand that I *lived* on the lanai.

How strange. As if I wouldn't come back on my own. Where else would I go? The comfy couch, the warm laps, the endless supply of yummy dinners—of course, I'd return. But their logic? Now *that* was silly.

Finally, Mom and Dad decided I had spent enough time confined to the lanai. The wait had felt endless, and I was starting to go stir-crazy, pacing back and forth across the screened enclosure. Beyond it stretched our sprawling backyard—a vast, untamed paradise teeming with squirrels, birds, and who knew what other exciting creatures just waiting to be chased. My paws itched with anticipation, my tail flicking impatiently. Would they ever set me free?

One afternoon, after what felt like an eternity of waiting, I overheard Mom and Dad deep in discussion, their voices low and serious. They were debating whether "it was time." My ears perked up; my heart pounded—could this be it? Finally, after what seemed like another lifetime, Dad reached for the door and held it open.

Like a coiled spring, I exploded forward, launching myself across the threshold with the speed of a wild leopard. My paws barely touched the ground as I streaked across the yard, the wind whipping through my fur. Then, I spotted it—a towering tree, its sturdy trunk calling to me like a challenge. Without hesitation, I bolted toward it and, in one powerful surge, scaled its rough bark, climbing higher and higher until I was at least twenty-five feet up.

I clung there for a moment, feeling the rush of freedom pulse through me. Every muscle in my body buzzed with pent-up energy—I had been waiting for this moment for what felt like forever. And now, finally, I was free.

And then, at that very moment, I knew for sure—my Dad was absolutely ridiculous. As I perched high in the tree, feeling like the king of the world, I heard him turn to Mom and say, completely serious, **"Go on, climb up and get him down."**

What?! Did he really think Mom could scale this tree like I had? I glanced down, half-expecting to see her gearing up for the impossible. But come on—she didn't have claws; she wasn't built for this! My tail flicked with amusement. Was Dad actually suggesting that my human, with her two legs and zero climbing skills, was going to shimmy up this tree like a squirrel?

I almost laughed. If cats could laugh, that is.

From my lofty perch, I took in the world like never before. The backyard stretched out beneath me, a vast playground of swaying grass, rustling bushes, and darting critters. The air was crisp and filled with the scent of adventure. I was exactly where I wanted to be—high above it all, the undisputed ruler of my domain.

But the real entertainment? That was happening below. Mom and Dad stood at the base of the tree, their heads tilted back, their voices filled with concern and confusion. They gestured, pointed, and debated in hushed but urgent tones, as if devising some grand rescue mission. I flicked my tail in amusement. Rescue? From what?

In my mind, there was nothing to figure out. No problem to solve. I had claimed my spot fair and square. I was free, I was untouchable, and I had no intention of coming down anytime soon.

I lounged on my high perch, tail swishing lazily, thoroughly entertained by the spectacle below. Mom and Dad were in full-on panic mode, pointing, whispering, and calling out their best attempts at coaxing me down.

"Come on, buddy! You can do it!" Dad encouraged.

"Just climb down the same way you went up!" Mom said, as if that genius idea hadn't already been on loop in my head a hundred times.

I watched them with half-lidded eyes, pretending to consider their advice. But in truth, I was in no hurry. If I rushed down, there was a good chance they'd scoop me up and march me straight back to the lanai. No, I had to be strategic about this.

So, I took my time, stretching, shifting my weight, and testing different angles. Should I go down headfirst like a daring jungle cat? Or maybe back down slowly, one paw at a time, like an expert climber? Decisions, decisions.

Meanwhile, below, Mom and Dad continued their frantic pep talk, as if their words alone could will me down. Oh, how I loved making them squirm.

Finally, after thoroughly enjoying the show, I decided to make my grand descent. With the grace of a true feline athlete, I strutted down the tree, tail high, paws landing lightly on the bark as if I had done this a thousand times before. Each step was deliberate, each movement a display of my undeniable skill. And, of course, I made sure to meow dramatically on the way down—just to let Mom and Dad know how impressive I truly was.

As soon as my paws hit the ground, Mom lunged forward, hands outstretched, clearly thinking she could scoop me up and end my glorious moment of freedom. **Ha! Not a chance.**

With a flick of my tail and a sideways smirk, I took off like a lightning bolt. My legs stretched, my lungs filled with the crisp air, and I raced across the backyard like a wildcat finally released into the wild. From one end to the other, I tore through the grass, leaping over bushes, zigzagging for no reason other than the sheer joy of it.

I was unstoppable. I was free. And most importantly, I had won.

And so, with my paws back on solid ground and my spirit soaring higher than any tree, I claimed my victory.

I am Cooper—Master of the Backyard, Conqueror of Trees, and the cat who always, always has the last laugh. ✍🐾

MEOW OUT

Cooper

Chapter 6: Cooper vs. The World: How I Trained My Humans During a Global Pandemic

Do you remember the days of—what was it called? Oh yeah, I think *COVID.*

Mom and Dad kept talking about it nonstop, and the TV was always on with the latest updates about the virus. "Flatten the curve," they'd say. "Social distancing," they'd whisper like it was some kind of top-secret code. Honestly, I thought it sounded like a new yoga pose.

I didn't understand much, so I asked my animal friends if they knew what was going on. Of course, they said no. We don't exactly get the morning news piped into the backyard.

But the one thing they *did* know was that all the humans were suddenly staying close to home. My buddy Max, the golden retriever next door, said it was like a dream come true. "They're home *all the time!*" he barked with a big, goofy grin. "I get three walks a day now. *Three!* I don't even have time to nap properly anymore!"

Even the cats were kind of into it. Lucy, the old tabby from down the street, said her humans were baking so much bread that she loved sleeping on top of the oven to stay warm. And don't even get me started on the squirrels—they were THRIVING. Less traffic meant more time for acorn treasure hunts.

As for me, I noticed things slowed down. No more rushed mornings with shoes flying everywhere and Mom spilling coffee as she tried to get out the door. Nope. Now it was long mornings with pancakes, slippers, and belly rubs. I mean, it was a little weird, sure—but kind of wonderful, too.

It was odd, sure, but the upside? In the middle of that quiet madness, the humans quit running. For once, they weren't just passing through; they started noticing. Us. The world. The tiny things that usually slide by unseen. And for a cat like me? That's what you call a *win.*

I noticed Max being walked nonstop. I mean, that guy was basically doing a full cardio routine every day. Up the street, down the street, over to the park, back again. Tongue hanging out, tail wagging like a flag in a hurricane—he was living his best life. And it wasn't just Max. The other dogs in the neighborhood were finally getting their daily dose

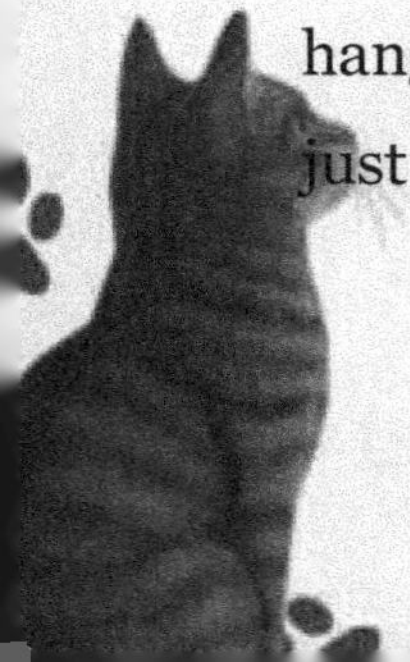

of exercise, too. Even Daisy, the tiny Chihuahua who usually preferred sunbathing on a pillow, was strutting down the sidewalk like she owned it.

Now, we all know cats don't do leashes or walks. That's beneath them. Lucy, the tabby, just sat on her windowsill, giving us all that signature look of judgment only a cat can give. You're all idiots," her gaze sneered, "and no, I'm not joining your little disaster parade.

But I was starting to wonder... was I missing out on something? Mom and Dad had started walking every day now. Not just a quick stroll either—these were *long* walks. Over an hour! They'd leave with smiles and come back looking even happier, like they'd discovered a hidden treasure. I'd watch from the lanai, tail thumping slowly, my eyes tracking their every move down the driveway.

Then one day, Mom came home with something new. She held it up like it was a prize: a leash. A red one. Just my color.

Yeah, right, I thought. *Me? A leash?*

But I let her clip it on, mostly out of curiosity—and okay, maybe a little bit of love. She looked so hopeful. The moment it clicked into place, though, I bolted like a rocket. I ran like the wind, ears flapping, paws pounding the ground like thunder. Poor Mom had no chance. That leash slipped right through her fingers, and I was off—faster than Max, faster than the mailman's truck, faster than whatever was making that weird buzzing noise by the fence.

I wasn't trying to escape. I was just... *free.*

That's when I realized something big was happening. The world was quieter, the people were closer, and even though everything felt different, in that moment, leash trailing behind me and the wind in my fur—I felt like I was part of something kind of special.

I looked back and saw Mom standing there, leash in hand, looking... well, *crushed.* Not in a dramatic way—she's not a cat, after all—but I could tell she was disappointed. And I didn't like that.

She's my top pick. Shh, don't tell Dad. I fake fairness, but of course I've got a favorite, what cat doesn't?

So, I did something completely out of character: I turned around and *ran* to her. Me—Cooper. Running *toward* a human. She knelt down, her face lighting up with surprise as I brushed against her legs like it had been my idea all along. She unhooked the leash gently, like we were silently agreeing never to speak of it again.

A moment passed. A truce was formed.

Later that afternoon, I saw her and Dad getting ready for their now-daily ritual: *The Walk*. Shoes. Sunglasses. That annoying clatter of keys. They were clearly gearing up for adventure.

I perched myself by the door, tail wrapped neatly around my paws, and stared up at them like, *"You forgot someone."*

Mom looked at me, puzzled. "You wanna come with us?"

I didn't blink. I didn't meow. I just gave her *The Look*. The one that says: *Of course I do. I am Cooper. I go where I please.*

No leash. No crate. No drama. Just me, padding along beside them like I was leading a royal procession.

I may be a cat, but I walked by their side that day.

Walking as a cat is an art form. Not everyone can pull it off—certainly not dogs, with their flailing tongues and frantic tail wagging. No, a proper walk requires intention, grace, and above all, *dignity*.

Cooper-style.

I didn't just *walk*—I *glided*. I paused often. Not because I was tired—please—but because observing is half the point. What's the use of leaving the house if you're not going to judge the world properly?

The neighborhood looked different that day. I'd spent years looking at it as I ran from the local raccoons, but being out on it, paws to pavement? That was next-level intel.

First stop: The Johnsons' yard. A squirrel darted up the tree, chattering at me like I'd personally offended his whole family. I stared back without blinking. That's right, pal—this sidewalk is mine now.

Then there was the house with the garden gnome. Hideous. I gave it a long glare, tail flicking disapprovingly. Mom thought I was interested. She crouched beside me, cooing like I was being cute. No, Mom—I'm being *critical.*

We passed Max the dog, who was on walk number three for the day and looked deliriously happy. He tried to say hi, bouncing up and down like a tennis ball with legs. I stopped. Sat. Looked him dead in the eyes and blinked slowly.

Cat speaks for: *Settle down, buddy. It's not that serious.*

I never rushed. Never strayed. And I *never* let them think they were in charge. I led the route with the confident air of someone who knew where we were going—even when I didn't. I often stopped mid-sidewalk and stared at nothing in particular, just to keep them guessing.

Every so often, I'd stroll into someone's yard like I owned it, sniff the base of a tree, then pivot dramatically and strut back to the sidewalk like a fashion model at the end of a runway.

People stopped to watch. They pointed. "Is that a *cat* on a walk?"

Yes. Yes, it is. Try to keep up.

We seemed to walk *forever.* I mean, I'm not complaining—I have excellent stamina for a cat—but let's be real, anything longer than twenty minutes and we're pushing into "epic quest" territory.

And then... it happened.

We crossed the *Big Street.*

Now, I'd seen it from the car window a few times. The one with the white lines painted across it, cars zipping by like they had somewhere more important to be than watching for elegant feline pedestrians. The *Big Street* was the edge of my known universe. Beyond it? Untamed land. Mystery. Chaos. Possibly raccoons.

Mom looked both ways like she always does—very responsible—and then we all stepped into the crosswalk together. I stayed right between her and Dad, very official, like I was a dignitary being escorted by my royal guard. Cars actually *stopped* to let us pass.

I gave one of the drivers my slow blink of approval. You're welcome, peasant.

Once we reached the other side, everything was new. The sidewalks smelled different. The grass was somehow *greener*. A breeze carried the scent of something delightful—was it chicken? I couldn't tell, but I made a mental note to return.

I paused dramatically in the middle of a stranger's driveway, sat down, and took it all in. The squirrels here were bolder. The birds are louder. One even chirped at me from a power line like it knew I wasn't allowed to climb up there. (For now.)

Adventure? Conquered. Big Street? Crossed. Cooper? Unstoppable.

Mom and Dad looked so *proud* of themselves. Beaming like they'd just solved world peace or won some parenting award. I heard Mom say, "Can you believe it? We've *tamed* him."

Yeah right.

Let's get one thing straight: I was never tamed. I *allowed* this arrangement. Big difference.

Sure, I walk beside them now. But make no mistake—I'm not some retriever eager to please. I'm a cat. A majestic, opinionated, highly evolved being who simply saw an opportunity for fresh air, mild entertainment, and perhaps an occasional breeze that ruffles my fur just so.

If anything, *I've* trained *them*. They know the pace now—slow, with plenty of stopping for "important investigations." They've learned to carry treats, to watch for shady resting spots, and to never—*ever*—try to pick me up mid-walk.

But I'll let them have their moment. I mean, if it makes them happy to think they tamed me, fine. I'll even throw in a soft purr when we get home. Let them think they've won.

It's good for morale.

Until next time, stay majestic, stay mysterious... and remember: I'm not following them—I'm leading. ✍🐾

Meow Out 🐾

Cooper

Chapter 7: Carrier of Doom and the Throne of Betrayal

Well, I knew the day would come. The Day of Abandonment. Again.

You try not to think about it when things are good—when your kibble bowl is always full, your sunbeam hits just right across the lanai rug, and your people—Mom and Dad—are dependable sources of chin scratches and warm laps. But when your first family drops you off at the shelter like yesterday's newspaper, you carry a quiet worry in the twitch of your tail: *Will it happen again?*

Lately, there had been whispers. Suspicious activity. Suitcases mysteriously appeared in the hallway—those awful zippered boxes with wheels, always harbingers of doom. Mom kept folding things and saying, "Don't forget sunscreen." Dad talked about flights and rental cars. They kept saying a certain word: "the vacation."

Now, let me just pause right there.

Vacation? We cats don't know that word. We don't need it. We *are* the vacation. Every day. Every moment. Our entire existence is one long luxurious lounge. While humans go scrambling off to "destress," we perfect the art of zen on top of laundry piles, in windowsills, and under beds. What could a "vacation" possibly give them that my majestic presence does not?

So yes—I had a feeling. A twinge in my whiskers. A flick in my ear. Something was happening. I started making extra passes through their legs, yowling just a bit louder in the mornings. Strategic guilt-tripping. I even batted my favorite mouse toy at Dad's foot with a flourish, hoping to stir some sentiment. *Remember me? I'm adorable. I'm irreplaceable. Don't you dare.*

And then... *it* appeared.

The *Cat Carrier of Doom.*

I hadn't seen it in months, maybe years in cat time (which, as you know, moves differently—more dramatically). But the moment it emerged from the shadowy back corner of the closet, I felt it in my soul. A cold, creeping dread slithered up my spine and made my whiskers tremble.

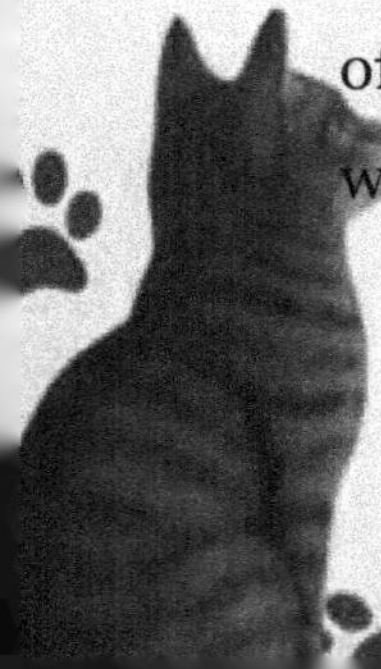

There it was: that plastic, grated, dungeon-on-the-go. Beige. Worn. Smelling faintly of betrayal and antiseptic. It wobbled slightly as Mom set it on the ground, as if it, too, was eager to consume me whole. The very *sound* of it—*click-thud*—sent a shiver down my magnificent tail.

Mom approached slowly, like I was some kind of naïve rookie. She crouched low and put on her "sweet voice"—you know the one, syrupy and high-pitched, usually reserved for toddlers and the vet's office.

"Coooooper," she sang, like I was about to get a massage and cucumber water. "Come on, sweetheart, hop in, just a little ride, promise."

Just hop in? Lady, I may eat bugs, but I wasn't born yesterday.

My instincts kicked in. I assessed my environment like a feline James Bond: two exits, one sun-drenched patio, one open screen door. I tensed my haunches, narrowed my eyes, and—*launch sequence initiated.*

I ran. No, I *flew* like a cheetah possessed. Around the pool, over the patio chairs, under the herb planter, with the speed and agility of a cat who's watched enough National Geographic to know what comes next.

Mom chased after me, waving a treat like it was a peace offering, yelling things like, "Cooper! Stop! You're being ridiculous!"

Ridiculous? Me? *Excuse* me, ma'am—I am executing a tactical evasion maneuver, thank you very much.

Every time she got close, I added a little flair: a dramatic leap, a backward glance of disdain, a tail flick that said, "Not today, woman." I made sure to run directly in front of the neighbor's fence so that the golden retriever next door could witness my performance. (He barked in appreciation. He gets it.)

And all of a sudden, I saw it. A flicker in Mom's eyes, like a candle sputtering in the wind.

She gave up.

She turned to Dad and said, her voice flat and defeated, "I guess we just have to leave him by himself."

What? *What?!*

My tail bristled. My ears twitched in disbelief.

I wasn't some feral kitten in an alley, dodging trash can lids and living off stale pizza crusts.

I was a cat of standards. Of dignity. Of *palate*.

Leave *me*? Alone? To fend for myself?

Gary, my friend the squirrel, might be good at cracking acorns and causing general chaos in the yard—but could he find me lobster mac and cheese? Could he heat it to the perfect temperature, with that golden, crispy cheese top?

No.

Gary once tried to drag half a granola bar into my bed like it was treasure.

This was not happening. I narrowed my eyes. I had survived the shelter. I had survived the vacuum monster. I *would not* be abandoned now, not when I had only just trained these humans to scratch behind my ears at the right angle.

So, with the dramatic flair of a feline martyr, I climbed into the Cat Carrier of Doom. Yes, *voluntarily*. Sometimes, a cat has to take fate by the whiskers.

The humans seemed stunned. Probably assumed I'd put up the usual battle—claws in the carpet, evasive maneuvers under the bed, a few well-timed yowls. But not today. I had to keep them guessing.

Then—*vroom*.

We were off. The car roared to life and hurled us down the street at what I can only describe as *excessive* speed. I pressed my nose against the carrier grate, fur fluffed from the sheer velocity. It felt like we were on a one-way trip to Mars.

My ears flattened with every bump and turn. My dramatic sighs went unacknowledged. Unbelievable.

Finally, we screeched to a halt. Tires squealed, brakes whined, and my stomach did a graceful somersault.

The door opened. A new smell—antiseptic, fur, and faint desperation.

Oh no.

The Vet.

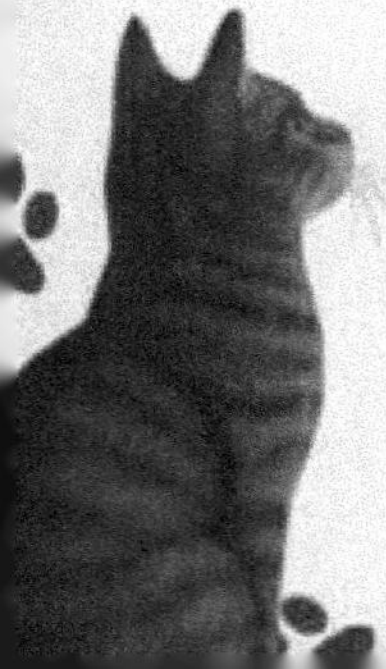

A new office. New smells. New forms of betrayal.

I braced myself, tail puffed, ears alert. I knew what was coming. The needle. The thermometer. Possibly that indignity of being weighed like a common sack of potatoes.

Still inside the carrier, I narrowed my eyes and reminded myself:

You are Cooper. You are sleek. You are crafty.

And if anyone tries to touch your paws, you *claw*.

I was carried—gently, suspiciously gently—into a bright room with actual windows. *Windows!*

Not the usual sterile exam room with steel tables and the scent of betrayal baked into the walls.

This room had a *huge climbing toy.* I mean, we're talking the Ritz-Carlton of cat trees. Carpeted ramps, sisal posts, hidey-holes, and best of all—a lofty perch that overlooked a sun-drenched window. From up there, I could see trees, a bird feeder, and what I assumed was Gary the squirrel casing the parking lot. Classic Gary.

My whiskers twitched.

What kind of vet was this?

The Cat Carrier of Doom creaked open—*slowly,* like they were defusing a bomb. I waited a beat, then made my move.

With the grace of a jungle panther (if jungle panthers were nine pounds and fluffy), I *leapt* out—ignoring the humans entirely—and launched myself onto the climbing tower. Scramble, stretch, *hop*.

And then—*perch*.

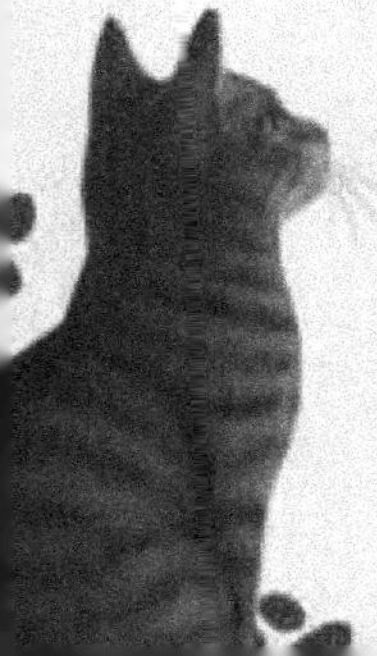

I sat at the top, surveying my kingdom. The view was excellent. The sun hit my fur just right. I was a majestic beast surveying my realm from a throne of sisal.

The humans watched in awe. Probably whispering things like, "What a magnificent creature," or "Should we cancel the exam and just let him live here?"

Honestly, not a bad idea.

But I knew better. This was a trap wrapped in luxury.
minute now, someone was going to sneak up behind me with a thermometer or a syringe the size of a baguette.

So I stayed alert. Regal, yes—but ready to flee at the first sign of treachery.

Until next time,

Stay fluffy, stay fierce, and never trust a closed door. ✍🐾

MEOW OUT

Cooper

Chapter 8: The Great Escape: A Tail of Feline Brilliance and Office Conquest

Ah. The door shut with that dreadful, definitive *click*, and suddenly I was alone. Along with the cat tower. The beige, carpeted monolith that stood in the corner like some kind of smug monument to feline imprisonment. It had three levels, two fuzzy mice dangling limply from frayed strings, and one sad little cubbyhole that smelled like disinfectant and fear. A "tower," they call it—please. I call it *Purgatory in Polyester*.

They thought they were clever. Sneaking out while I was mid-tail-flick? Amateurs. I *knew* this was going to happen the moment I saw Mom put that tiny suitcase in the car—the one she uses when she's abandoning me for more than twelve hours. She tried to play it cool, all scratch-behind-the-ear and baby-voice, "Oh, Cooper, you're gonna be *so* well taken care of," but I caught the twitch in her eye. The guilt. The betrayal. Classic.

But it wasn't until I heard the vet say the words—those *terrible* words—that I realized the full extent of the horror.

"He'll be taken care of for the next few days."

Excuse me, *what*?

Taken care of?

Taken care of?

That's mob talk. That's what happens to witnesses in crime dramas who know too much. And in this case, *I* knew too much—like where Mom keeps the snacks, and what time she really gets home from "yoga."

And then it hit me.

This was a sleepover.

At. The. Vet.

I have never had a sleepover at the vet before. I don't *do* sleepovers unless there's gourmet pâté, feather toys, and at least one warm lap involved. And certainly not in a place where everyone wears rubber gloves and smells faintly of iodine and broken dreams.

I slinked to the edge of the cat tower and gave it a good sniff. Yup. The previous occupant had clearly lost all hope. Probably left a last will and testament scratched into the underside of the top platform.

I jumped up to the middle level and flopped dramatically, limbs hanging like overcooked noodles. This was it. I was a prisoner of war. I was Mewlius Caesar, betrayed by those I trusted most.

And still... There was a little part of me—just a tiny flicker of curiosity—that wondered what kind of snacks they kept hidden behind those cold steel drawers. Because if I were stuck here for *days*, I was going to need a strategy.

This was no longer a sleepover. This was *survival.*

I was able to entertain myself for the next few hours—*barely*. The cat tower, while beneath my standards, did offer a few distractions. I batted halfheartedly at one of the limp toys (whose spirit, much like mine, had clearly been broken long ago) and climbed to the top tier to peer through the small glass window in the door, the one that made me feel like I was in some kind of fuzzy feline fishbowl.

Humans wandered by on the other side. Their white coats and squeaky shoes betrayed their intentions. They passed my door like I was some sort of exotic exhibit at a second-rate zoo. *"Ooh, look, it's a domestic shorthair with resting judgment face!"* Yes, Brenda. I see you. I am judging your bangs.

Every now and then, one of them would enter the room with forced enthusiasm and the kind of chirpy voice usually reserved for toddlers and unstable parrots.

"Hi there, Cooper! You're doing *so* well! Dinner's at six, sweet boy!"

Six? Excuse me, madam, I dine at five thirty. With candles and soft jazz. Not in some sterile fish bowl.

Each attempt at petting was met with my signature reception: a sideways glare, one strategic tail flick, and just the faintest narrowing of my pupils. I wasn't rude—I was *dignified*. There's a difference. And while I did allow one intern a brief chin stroke, it was only because her hands smelled like tuna and I was weak.

I was not going to be real friendly at the start of this visit. No, sir. They needed to earn it. Earn *me*. I wasn't here to make friends. I was here to survive the great betrayal, plot my eventual return, and maybe steal a packet of treats if left unattended.

By 5:59, I was poised near the door, like a panther waiting in the reeds. If this so-called "dinner" didn't meet my expectations, I had every intention of staging a protest—possibly involving tipped water bowls and dramatic yowling.

After dinner was served—*if* you can call that flavorless pile of mystery mush "dinner" (seriously, was it turkey? was it tuna? was it *packing foam*?)—I gave it a sniff, a pause for dramatic effect, and then begrudgingly took a few bites. A gentleman must maintain his strength, even in captivity.

Then it happened. The unmistakable shift in tone. Doors clicking. Keys jangling. Voices calling out their goodbyes. The humans were *leaving*. One by one, they vanished, like the sun disappearing behind a cloud of indifference.

Then the lights went out.

Total darkness.

For most creatures, this would be cause for alarm—maybe even a little whimpering, some nervous pacing. But not for me. Oh no. I was built for this.

You see, I have *night vision.*

Not to brag (okay, a little), but my retinas are equipped with a tapetum lucidum, which is Latin for *I can see you sneaking that extra cookie in the kitchen at 2 a.m., Susan*. The room that seemed so cold and clinical during the day became my midnight kingdom.

I jumped silently down from the tower and prowled the floor like a panther on patrol. My whiskers guided me along the baseboards, and I discovered all sorts of secrets. A stray piece of kibble under the cat tower. A dust bunny with ambition. A discarded rubber glove was behind the waste bin that I batted around like a toy of questionable hygiene.

I paused in the center of the room, ears perked, tail high. The silence was rich. Delicious. No barking dogs. No loud TVs. No vacuum monster. Just me, the shadows, and the soft hum of the thermostat.

This wasn't a cage—it was my *fortress.*

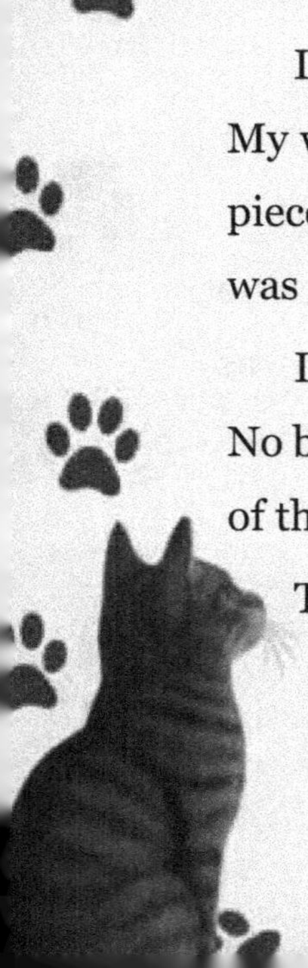

I leapt up onto the windowsill, positioned myself just so, and stared out into the night with the kind of gravitas normally reserved for movie posters. If anyone had walked by right then, they'd have seen my silhouette framed against the darkness, eyes glowing, majestic.

"He watches," they would whisper. *"The Chosen One."*

And they'd be right.

And then—somewhere between batting the crinkly toy into submission and staring wistfully at the exit—a brilliant idea sparked in my mind. A genius-level, paws-down *masterstroke.* To this day, I consider it one of my finest moments. Right up there with the time I faked a limp for three whole hours just to get out of bath day.

You see, I'd been watching that door handle. Observing it. Studying it like it was a mouse-shaped puzzle only I could solve. It was one of those lever handles, not a round one—*amateurs.* Practically begging to be manipulated by a determined feline with nothing to lose.

And I thought: *Cooper, my handsome devil, you've still got it.*

I sprang up to the top of the cat tower, tail twitching with purpose. I crouched low, like a jungle cat surveying the open plains—except my jungle smelled like antiseptic and someone else's litter box.

The plan was elegant in its simplicity: Leap. Smack the handle. Open sesame. Freedom.

Attempt #1: I misjudged the launch angle and merely grazed the wall, landing with an undignified thud that echoed off the tile. I licked my shoulder for exactly eight seconds to recover my pride.

Attempt #2: Better trajectory, but I hit the handle with the wrong paw. It jiggled. *It jiggled!* My heart soared. *Progress!* Then the door stayed shut, and I made a noise that was somewhere between a growl and a disappointed sigh.

Attempt #3: A near miss. I swatted the handle just as my back paw slipped off the edge of the tower. I landed in the water bowl. It splashed. I sulked. I may have muttered something impolite under my breath.

But Attempt #4?

Attempt #4 was *poetry*.

I launched with the precision of a gymnast and the ferocity of a creature who had been denied a proper dinner and subjected to patronizing chin rubs. My paw hit the handle *square on*. It moved—*gloriously, creakily moved*—and with a soft click that might as well have been a choir of angels, the door *opened*. Just a crack, but enough.

I landed like a ninja. Ears up. Tail frozen mid-wave. Did anyone hear? Was I caught?

Silence.

And just like that, I was free.

The hallway stretched out before me like a glowing path of opportunity. My whiskers tingled. My pupils widened. I was Cooper: Escape Artist. Legend. Myth.

The office was now my *kingdom.*

Every filing cabinet, every swivel chair, every scent-smeared corner was mine to explore and claim. I slinked through the corridors like a shadow wrapped in fur, tail held high, the very embodiment of stealth and sophistication. I leapt onto desks, leaving perfectly formed paw prints on clean reports. I danced across keyboards, probably sending an email or two. (If someone in billing received a message that read, "rrrrrrrftttttttttttttt," you're welcome.)

I discovered a basket of pens that I joyfully knocked over one by one. I perched on the copy machine like a lion on the savannah, silently daring it to move. I found a cabinet left slightly ajar and crawled inside to investigate its contents, which turned out to be mostly paperclips and despair.

The breakroom? Divine. A haven of smells: old tuna salad, forgotten crackers, and the lingering aroma of someone's over-microwaved spaghetti. I hopped onto the counter, gave the coffeepot a disdainful sniff (how do they *drink* that stuff?), and batted a sugar packet off the edge just for fun.

It *felt* like minutes—glorious, uninterrupted minutes of freedom and conquest—but I know now it had to have been hours. Time works differently when you're victorious.

Then it happened.

The jingling of keys. The sound of human voices returning, cheerful and caffeinated. I froze mid-prowl behind the printer, my tail giving one satisfied twitch. Oh, this was going to be *good.*

The door opened, and in they came, chatting and yawning and expecting, I don't know, *obedience.* They turned to my little room—my former cell—and gasped. The door was ajar. The cat tower was empty.

"Where's Cooper?"

Where's Cooper, indeed?

I emerged from behind the front desk with all the slow, smug drama of a magician revealing the grand finale. Their eyes went wide. One of them dropped her keys. Another let out a little shriek. I sat down calmly in the middle of the hallway, licked my paw, and gave them a look that said, *Amateurs. Truly.*

"Oh no," one whispered. "Did someone leave the door open last night?"

Yeah, sure, Janice. Keep telling yourself that. Ignore the paw prints stamped like signatures on the mini fridge and the faint gouge in the handle, etched there in the perfect curve of my claws. Denial is a cozy little lie the clueless wrap themselves in.

They scooped me up with the nervous reverence one might reserve for royalty found wandering the grounds. I allowed it. I had nothing to prove. My legend had already been written in toner dust and discarded sticky notes.

I kept to myself that day, regal, aloof, and utterly *glorious*. I lounged in my cell (which now felt more like a private suite), tail curled just so, grooming one paw with slow satisfaction. Inside, I was practically cackling. I had pulled off the *heist of the century*, and no one even knew it.

The humans were fluttering around more than usual, peeking in on me like I might pull another vanishing act at any moment. Their footsteps were faster, their voices a little higher-pitched, like nervous pigeons circling a park bench.

"Oh, he's resting—poor thing must've been so stressed!"

Stressed? *Please*. I was basking in the glow of my own genius.

They tried the usual nonsense—"Who's a good boy?" and "Wanna chin rub?"—but I simply turned the other way, presenting my most elegant shoulder blade. I didn't even

flinch when they tried the trick where they dangle a feather like it's 2009, and I don't see the string. I had *standards* now. I was a legend in my own time.

I spent the afternoon cycling between my tower's top tier and a sunbeam that moved slowly across the floor, which I claimed as mine and mine alone. I napped like a king: one eye half open, just in case opportunity knocked again.

Then came quitting time.

I could tell by the bustle, the zip of bags being zipped, the sound of the snack drawer being ransacked one last time. The lights began to flicker off, one by one, casting long, lazy shadows across the walls. I watched silently from my perch as the humans shuffled out, calling their goodbyes.

"Night, Cooper!"

I didn't respond. Not even a blink.

The last light clicked off. The place fell into stillness.

Darkness again.

But this time, it was different. This time, I wasn't a confused prisoner wondering how I'd survive the night.

This time, I was the *phantom of the office*. A myth. A whisper in the breakroom. The reason janitors double-check the locks is.

I stretched luxuriously, letting one claw extend with theatrical flair.

Let the games begin.

And I *did* the exact same things every night I was there. Same leap from the top of the cat tower, same flawless handle smack, same stealthy slide into the forbidden world beyond the door. It became my routine—my midnight ritual.

Night falls.

Freedom calls.

Cooper answers.

I believe it was three nights... maybe four. Who knows? Time is a construct, especially when you're busy ruling your secret kingdom under the cover of darkness.

Each night, I re-explored the office like a king returning to survey his lands. I patrolled the hallways. Reclaimed the breakroom. Left my paw print on exactly one file folder in the corner office, just to let them know I'd been there. I even knocked over the same sugar packet. Ritual is important.

And every morning, I returned—flawlessly—to my tower, poised and composed, as if nothing had happened. I'd be grooming my paw like a model on a chaise lounge by the time the first human opened the front door. Not a hair out of place. Just the faint scent of copier toner in my fur. But the door to my kingdom would always be open.

The best part?

The vet. Oh, the *vet*.

She could not believe it. Flabbergasted. Bewildered. Distracted in the middle of checking a golden retriever's gums, just trying to figure out how *the cat* kept getting out. I watched her pacing in the hallway, arms folded, muttering to herself while one of the techs nervously fiddled with a clipboard.

"I swear we locked it."

"Was the latch broken?"

"Could someone be playing a prank?"

Blaming the techs left and right. *HA!*

I watched from my perch, eyes half-lidded, tail flicking just slightly. If only they knew. If only they understood the genius that lurked behind these expressive whiskers and majestic paws.

But they didn't.

And that's just how I liked it.

The day finally came—at last—when Mom returned.

I heard her voice before I saw her, that familiar musical tone that always carried treats, chin rubs, and the subtle promise of dignity. My ears perked. My whiskers twitched. I leapt down from my tower with the kind of enthusiasm usually reserved for laser pointers and rogue moths.

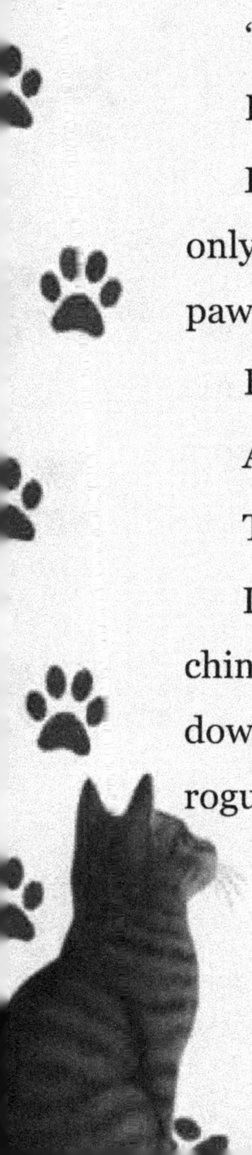

And there she was. Mom. In the flesh. Radiating love, comfort, and the faint scent of laundry detergent and cheese snacks.

I may or may not have let out a slightly undignified chirp. I may or may not have launched myself into her arms like a dramatic Victorian heroine. And yes, I even purred. Loudly. Like a motorboat driven by joy.

She clutched the Cat Carrier of Doom in her hands—the same one I had hissed at during our last vet-bound voyage—but in that moment, I greeted it like an old frenemy. Because it meant one thing: I was going home.

I gave her my most exaggerated nuzzle, bumping my head into her chin, flicking my tail just so. She laughed and kissed my ears and called me her "silly escape artist." Oh, if only she knew.

And then, as she spoke with the vet, I heard it. The line that sealed my legacy:

"I'm sorry, but Cooper won't be allowed to have any more sleepovers here," the vet said, her voice laced with a mixture of awe and exhaustion. "He seems to be able to... well... escape the room. In all my years, I've never seen anything like it."

Never, she said.

Never in her years.

Oh, how my heart sang.

I turned slightly, just enough for her to catch a glint of triumph in my eye. No words. Just legend.

Mom tucked me into the carrier, and I didn't even protest. Not a single meow. I sat proudly, tail wrapped around my paws, knowing that the office would whisper about me long after I was gone. The staff would tell tales of the clever gray cat who conquered doors and outwitted the best of them.

And as we drove home, I purred the whole way—low and steady. I was going back to my castle, my comforts, and my properly scheduled five-thirty dinners.

But deep down, I knew:

They would never forget me.

Stay clever, stay curious, and always keep one paw on the door handle. ✍🐾

MEOW OUT

Purrs and triumph,

Cooper

Escape Artist. Legend. Cat.

Chapter 9: Dry Paws & Wet Fools

You may not believe this, but cats do listen and pay attention to their surroundings. We're not just loafing around like furry lumps—we're surveillance experts. Experts, I tell you.

Take Mom, for example. She loves what I call *splashing in the pool*. It's not graceful, it's not coordinated, and it's definitely not something I'd ever voluntarily do. She calls it "swimming," but from my vantage point on the patio chair, it looks more like she's being chased by invisible jellyfish. She moves from one side of the pool to the other, arms flailing, legs kicking, water sloshing everywhere. Frankly, it's chaos. I've thought about calling a lifeguard more than once, but apparently, she "knows what she's doing." Hmm. Debatable.

And don't even get me started on the *soundtrack* to this aquatic drama. She cranks up the volume to levels that rattle my whiskers. Beach Boys. Jimmy Buffett. Occasionally, some Kenny Chesney is thrown in for extra flavor. It's like a tropical luau crashed into a surfboard shop and decided to stay forever. Look, I get it—humans love their tunes—but I swear if I hear *"Margaritaville"* one more time, I might pack a tiny suitcase and head for quieter litter.

But here's the thing—I watch her. I listen. Because despite all the splashing and singing and questionable dance moves on the pool deck, she's *my* human. And I've got her back. From a dry, elevated, safe-from-splash-zone distance, of course.

Sometimes Dad comes out to the pool wearing what can only be described as a blindingly loud shirt. Bright flowers—pink, yellow, orange—exploding all over it like someone let a toddler go wild with a paint set. I tried to ask him about it one day. I gave him *the look*, you know, that slow blink with a head tilt. The universal feline expression for *Are you sure about this?*

But instead of rethinking his fashion choices, he just laughed and told Mom he wore it because he heard her singing *"Good Vibrations"* from inside the house and he "wanted to get in on the fun." Now, I'm no expert on human courtship rituals, but what happened next was... something.

Without warning, Mom leapt out of the pool like a dolphin late for a concert. Water flew everywhere—my tail barely survived the spray. She started swinging her arms around like she was conducting an invisible Beach Boys orchestra. Then her feet got in on the action—somewhere between a cha-cha and someone hopping across hot pavement.

Dad, not to be outdone, joined in. There they were, two adults, one dripping wet and wildly flailing in what I assume they believed to be a dance. To me, it looked like they were being attacked by invisible bees. But they were laughing, spinning in circles, and even doing some kind of synchronized finger pointing like they were in a music video filmed entirely in a Jimmy Buffett-themed gift shop.

Meanwhile, I perched in my usual observation post—on the dry lounge chair, thank you very much—with one paw elegantly tucked under and the other holding up my dignity. I watched the whole scene unfold like some bizarre mating ritual from a Discovery Channel documentary.

I must say, it was confusing. No treats involved, no toys, and they were voluntarily *wet*. But still, I couldn't help but purr a little. Because even though it looked ridiculous—Dad with his technicolor shirt and Mom doing interpretive splash dance moves—it was kind of beautiful in its own strange, human way. They were happy. Genuinely happy.

And happiness, my friends, is contagious—even to us aloof, superior beings.

Just don't expect me to join in. I've got limits. And water is one of them.

Dad said something the other day—between gulps of lemonade and attempts at dancing—that really stuck with me. He leaned back in one of those creaky pool loungers, still wearing that blinding shirt that could double as a traffic signal, and said, "Now *this* is the lifestyle. Beach Boys, pool, sunshine... doesn't get better than this."

I gave him a long, slow blink from my shady perch beneath the hibiscus plant. *Lifestyle?* Oh, *you* have a lifestyle, Dad? Cute.

Because, let me tell you, I've got a lifestyle that would make most creatures—feline, canine, or otherwise—absolutely green with envy.

Let's start with my morning routine. I wake up precisely when I want to, usually after the sun has risen and before Mom's made her first cup of coffee. No alarms. No traffic. No

meetings. Just a leisurely stretch, a luxurious yawn, and a dramatic roll onto my back to signal that yes, I am awake, and the world may resume spinning.

Then comes breakfast, served with just the right amount of ceremony. I've trained them well—Mom uses the special dish with the fish pattern I like, and she talks to me while she opens the can. Sure, I pretend I'm aloof, but I'm listening. Every word. Especially the ones like "chicken" and "tuna."

After that, I move into my mid-morning *chaise shift*—also known as *surveillance duty*. This is a high-ranking position in the household, not to be taken lightly. I perch on the chaise lounge—the one Mom insists is *hers*, but we all know the truth. I claimed it months ago with a well-placed fur nest and a few subtle claw punctures. Ownership, secured.

From this throne, I have a commanding view of the backyard and the community sidewalk. It's the perfect vantage point for observing *everything*. Joggers huffing by in neon shorts, determined dog walkers being dragged down the sidewalk by overzealous golden retrievers, garbage trucks rumbling like beasts from the underworld, and the occasional rogue squirrel performing acrobatics on the fence like it's auditioning for a circus.

Nothing escapes my gaze.

And if someone dares—*dares*—to walk a dog past *my* house? Oh, you better believe they're getting a warning glare. Not just any glare. This is the narrowed-eyes, still-as-a-statue, tail-twitching kind of stare that says, "You are on thin ice, furball." It's a finely tuned art. The humans think I'm just "watching." No. I am issuing silent but firm decrees of territorial dominance.

Sometimes I catch a little kid pointing at me from a stroller. I give them a brief nod of acknowledgment. You never know which of them may grow up to be a respectable cat servant. I believe in community outreach.

And if Mom comes by and sees me stretched out, basking in a sunbeam on her beloved chaise, she just sighs and says, "Well, you *look* busy, Cooper." Busy? I am *essential*. This house doesn't monitor itself.

Surveillance ends when the sun moves and my patch of light disappears. Time to move on.

Afternoons are for napping. Strategic, restorative naps—the kind that would make a spa jealous. I don't just *sleep*; I *curate* rest.

I rotate through my preferred locations based on the movement of the sun and the energy of the house. First stop: the back of the couch. It's high enough to oversee the room like a general on a velvet battlefield, with just the right amount of cushion-to-pool screen ratio. I curl into a perfect crescent, tail tucked just so, ears twitching occasionally at the distant sound of a passing lawn mower or someone unwrapping cheese in the kitchen.

When the sunbeam shifts—and trust me, I follow it with the precision of a feline sundial—I relocate. Sometimes it's the couch, where I can sink into a fortress of pillows and channel my inner monarch-in-hiding. Other times, I make a bold move to Mom's chaise chair by the door. It's soft, shady, and just bold enough to spark a little excitement. I nestle in deep, fully aware that I'll be "found out" eventually and escorted elsewhere. Totally worth it. And then there's my signature move: the *dramatic flop* on the cool lanai pavers. It's part performance art, part temperature regulation. I stretch to full length—limbs akimbo, belly exposed just enough to tempt but not enough to allow petting. This is not an invitation. This is a *statement*. A proclamation of my majestic presence. The humans can't help but comment. "Look at you, Cooper! You're living the life!" they coo.

Yes. Yes, I am.

Every nap is deliberate. Each stretch, a slow-motion display of elegance. I nap with intention. With purpose. I am the curator of calm, the ambassador of leisure. I am the feline embodiment of "do not disturb."

And don't worry—I still hear everything. The fridge opening, the rattle of a treat bag, the faintest whisper of Mom saying the word "vet." I may be still, but I am never unaware.

But rest assured, the moment a tail, paw, or unfamiliar shoe crosses my territory line again, I'll be back on duty. Vigilant. Watchful. Slightly annoyed.

Such is the burden of greatness.

So yes, Dad may have his Beach Boys and his splashy pool time. But me? I have sunbeams that follow me from chaise to couch to driveway, gourmet meals in tiny portions, and two full-grown humans wrapped around my delicate paw.

My lifestyle isn't accidental. It's curated, elevated, and, let's be real, untouchable..

I didn't choose the luxurious outdoor cat life—it chose me. And I wear it well.

Chapter 10: The Great Escape: Cooper Outsmarts the Wild

Mom and Dad started letting me out of the lanai every day, a decision I fully supported (and frankly, wondered why it had taken them so long). That's when the real adventure began—when I started to explore my new hood properly.

Our backyard was big—big enough for serious reconnaissance—and had a sort of untamed charm to it. Towering trees threw lazy shadows across the grass, their leaves whispering secrets to each other in the breeze. The fence at the far end wasn't just a fence—it was a border to the great unknown, separating our yard from a sprawling nature preserve. Beyond it, the world grew even wilder. I could hear it: the rustle of unseen critters in the underbrush, the sharp calls of birds high up in the trees, the occasional thud of something much larger moving just out of sight. It was exhilarating. It was chaos. It was perfect.

I padded through the yard like an explorer mapping a new continent. Every tuft of grass, every stubborn patch of weeds, every broken branch held the possibility of discovery. Sometimes I'd freeze, tail twitching, at the sound of a lizard scuttling across a rock or a squirrel daring to chitter at me from a low-hanging branch.

This wasn't just a backyard anymore. It was my kingdom.

One afternoon, I wandered farther than I ever had before, drawn by the scent of something fresh and cool. I padded over to a small stream tucked inside the preserve, not far from the edge of my backyard. The water shimmered under the late sun, rippling gently over smooth stones. I lowered my head and drank deeply, the coldness sharp and clean against my tongue. It tasted like adventure—like freedom.

Water down, mission up. Next on my agenda: tree shopping. I sniffed and scratched my way down the block, auditioning trunks left and right, each one judged by the gold standard of comfort: the ridiculously plush couch I once ruled. A tree would have to be just right if I were going to spend the night. None of this poky, scratchy nonsense.

Hours must have passed as I darted from tree to tree, my paws silent against the earth, my tail flicking with impatience. At last, I found it: a grand old tree standing gracefully in a clearing, its leaves whispering secrets to the wind. The bark was smooth enough to climb

but sturdy enough to hold me. I scampered up with effortless elegance, barely disturbing a single branch. At the top, a thick, perfect crook between two limbs cradled me like it had been waiting just for me.

I stretched luxuriously, curling into a tight ball, my fur ruffling slightly in the cool evening breeze. Sleep claimed me quickly.

And as I slept, dreams floated around me—whispers in the darkness. I heard Mom and Dad, their voices soft and pleading, "Come back, Cooper, come back." Their calls wrapped around me like a ghostly hug, tugging at my heart even as I slept.

When morning finally broke, I woke with a sharp pang of loneliness. No warm hands scratching behind my ears. No admiring coos over my perfect whiskers. No smell of pancakes wafting through the air. Just the empty, hollow sigh of the forest.

For a moment, sadness weighed heavy on me.

But then I remembered *that* place—the cold metal table, the awful lights, and worst of all, the fake smile the veterinarian gave me, all shiny teeth and bad intentions. No, I thought, shuddering. Never again. Freedom was worth the trade.

I was just beginning to plan my next grand exploration when it happened.

I was cornered in a tree on one of the smallest branches (which, to me, was still pretty big — like a highway for squirrels) with a coyote about to eat me. And when I say eat me, I don't mean in a metaphorical, "life's challenges are nibbling at my spirit" kind of way — I mean literal teeth, literal me. I was petrified. My heart was pounding so hard I was sure it was creating a low-frequency vibration only coyotes could hear.

I've never been attacked by a coyote before — or attacked by anything for that matter, unless you count that one time my cousin's parakeet went rogue — and I knew, eventually, I would die. But I didn't want to die like this. I always pictured my demise being far more dignified. You know, peacefully, maybe surrounded by loved ones, definitely not while squawking in a tree like some deranged housecat.

I sighed, a long, dramatic sigh — the kind you give when you realize your fate is entirely out of your hands. If this situation didn't improve soon, I was going to cry. Ugly cry. The coyote, completely unfazed by my emotional distress, kept creeping closer, his eyes locked on me like I was the last slice of pizza at a party.

As he approached, I noticed the branch beneath me starting to quiver. It was not built for this kind of action. The coyote was about six or seven feet away when the branch began making ominous creaking noises. You know that sound that trees make in horror movies, right before something terrible happens? Yeah, that.

The branch twisted and cracked, and just as the coyote took his final pounce — SNAP! The branch held on by a single strip of bark, and in a beautiful, synchronized moment of chaos, both the coyote and I plummeted to the ground.

Now, I'd like to tell you that I fell with grace, but no. I meowed. Loudly. I didn't know that was my instinctual distress sound, but apparently, it is. When I hit the ground, I sprang up so fast you'd think I had rocket boosters in my shoes.

The coyote was still sprawled out, stunned by either the fall or my incredibly unexpected feline impression. I didn't wait to find out. I took off like my life depended on it — because, you know, it did — running in the direction I believed my house was. Or at least some place with fewer coyotes and more snacks.

Victory.

Cooper: 1.

Coyote: 0.

And the best part? I couldn't wait to tell Max and Lucy that not only had I escaped a wild coyote, but I had *flown* through the air like a superhero doing it.

Because sometimes being clever isn't about being stronger or faster.

It's about thinking like a cat.

Until next time, stay clever, stay curious, and always land on your feet.

MEOW OUT

Cooper

Chapter 11: The Pool Incident: Tales of a Soaked Sovereign

Ah, yes—the pool.

Not just a splashy puddle like those tragic birdbaths our neighbors call "water features." No, no. *My* kingdom included a **real** swimming pool. Deep. Wide. Shimmering like a jeweled mirror under the sun. It was the crown jewel of my domain, my own private moat, and the greatest source of feline fascination and suspicion I had ever encountered.

It wrapped from one side of the lanai to the other. During the day, it glittered—a mosaic of blue tiles and moving light, the surface never still, always whispering little stories with its ripples. At night, it transformed into something else entirely: a glowing, mysterious portal that hummed under the moonlight, as if it knew secrets from the deep.

I often perched on the edge, tail curled neatly around my paws, gazing at it with what the humans called "deep concern." (What they fail to realize is that I was merely calculating the odds of an aquatic invasion. *You never know.*)

Once, a leaf landed on the surface, drifting like a tiny ship. I batted at it from the side and watched it glide away, smug in its inaccessibility. I considered leaping in—*briefly*. But let's not get carried away. I'm clever, not reckless. Water and fur have a complicated relationship.

Sometimes, I watched the humans use it. They'd leap in like overgrown otters, splashing, laughing, flailing their limbs in all directions like it was the height of joy. I'd sit nearby, judging. Supervising. Making sure no one drowned. (It would be a logistical nightmare for me if someone went under—no thumbs.)

My favorite time? Twilight.

That moment just after dinner when the sky turned lavender and the air smelled of jasmine and leftover barbecue. The lights around the pool would flicker on—soft and golden—and I'd stretch out on the warm pavers, belly to the sky, watching the water reflect the first stars. Peaceful. Majestic. Mine.

It wasn't just a pool.

It was *The Pool.*

A place of beauty. Mystery. Occasional bug chases.

And it was part of my glorious kingdom.

Mom had this routine—suspiciously stealthy for a human. Every morning, like clockwork, she'd slink out of bed without making a peep, as if she were avoiding a pack of sleeping wolves. No lights. No creaky floorboards. Just ninja-level silence.

She'd tiptoe to the lanai, flip on the glowing blue box (humans call it the TV, but I know better—it's obviously a portal to another world), and then—*SPLASH*—headfirst into the water like it was her personal baptism into sanity.

And then, the chaos began.

For the next thirty minutes, there'd be splashing, kicking, puffing, and that strange underwater flapping sound like a duck in distress. From my post on the edge of the jacuzzi —where I kept watch, as any respectable feline should—I observed the whole thing with a mixture of awe and judgment. I mean, who voluntarily throws themselves into water *every day*? Madness.

But this day? This day was different.

Halfway through her watery thrashing, Mom let out a yelp. A short, sharp *"OH!"*—like she'd been surprised mid-stroke. I bolted upright. Tail puffed, ears perked. Was it an alligator? A rogue noodle float? A malfunction in the glowing box portal system?

Turns out... it was me.

Unbeknownst to her, I was on the tiny edge of the Jacuzzi that was on the deep end of the pool. The tile was warm, the air was thick with chlorine, and honestly, I was curious. Why was she doing this every day? What was the appeal?

Well, just as she flipped into a backstroke turn, I leaned a *bit* too far forward to investigate. And wouldn't you know it—I slipped. One elegant paw dipped in, then another, and before I knew it... *KER-PLUNK.*

Full-body immersion.

The water was cold. The betrayal was real.

My yowl could be heard three neighborhoods away.

Mom shrieked and flailed, "COOPER?!", like *I* was the intruder. She scooped me up, wrapped me in a towel like some soggy burrito, and whispered apologies while laughing hysterically.

Dad, now wide awake thanks to the commotion, stumbled out, hair in full rooster mode. He blinked at us—Mom, dripping wet, cradling a soaked, furious feline—and muttered, "Well... that's one way to start the day."

Needless to say, I haven't been near the pool since. I prefer my adventures dry and my dignity intact. I've learned that tile is slippery, water is cold, and humans will *definitely* laugh at you when you look like a drowned squirrel. That was not one of my finer moments.

These days, I supervise Mom's swim sessions from a much safer distance—preferably behind the screened lanai door, where I can maintain proper hydration levels (i.e., 0%) and observe her aquatic rituals like the regal overlord I am. Occasionally, I toss in a meow of encouragement, just to let her know she's being watched. She says I'm "cheering her on," but really, I'm reminding her that she's splashing around in a giant water bowl and it's *very weird* behavior.

On the rare occasion she forgets my meal for the sake of her swim, I take my post by the towel basket and deliver the stare: deliberate, unblinking. The guilt settles in like a decree. Her laps shorten. One precise tail flick and the lesson is delivered. I've trained her to obey.

And then there's the matter of *The Net*. The long blue pole with the leaf-catching scoop on the end. She uses it to skim the surface of the pool. I use it as a prop in my highly choreographed sneak attacks. I'll stalk it from the shadows, leap onto the mesh, cling for dear life, and ride it like a flying dragon. It never gets old. The humans call it "hilarious." I call it *training*.

Because one day—one day—if that glowing box ever tries to swallow Mom, I'll be ready.

But for now, I stick to sunbeams, lanai lizards, and an occasional towel nap while she swims. It's safer that way. Drier too.

Besides, I've heard rumors of a new threat in the house... something called "Roomba." And that, my friends, is a tale for another day.

With fur slightly ruffled but pride mostly restored, ✍🐾

Meow Out 🐾
Cooper

Chapter 12: Dumpster Diving and the Rise of the Polka-Dot Patrol

One gloriously sunny afternoon, there I was—stretched out like royalty in my favorite sunbeam on the sidewalk—when *something* caught my sharp eye. About 20 feet away, right there in the driveway, stood a giant, ugly, metallic monster: a DUMPSTER.

An intruder.

A menace.

A possibly *very interesting* opportunity.

My ears perked up, my tail flicked with intrigue. Dad was pacing nearby, looking like he'd just found out his favorite scratching post had been thrown out. "I don't know why we had to get such a large one; we don't have that much stuff," he muttered, throwing bewildered glances at the hulking beast already half-stuffed with boxes and bags.

From my superior position on the sidewalk throne, I watched as the humans scurried about, hurling treasure into the abyss. My whiskers twitched with horror. Perfectly good treasures! A half-eaten toy mouse! A broken fountain! How could they *discard* such wonders??

I *had* to investigate.

No hesitation.

The time for lounging was over. The time for action had arrived.

Stealth mode: *activated.*

I slinked around the house, using every bit of my expert camouflage skills (a.k.a blending into random lawn debris). Inch by inch, I approached the beast, crouching low behind a pile of cardboard casualties. My heart pounded with excitement. What *secrets* might lie within?

Just as I prepared to leap, a flicker of gray caught my eye. Chuck the squirrel, casual as ever, perched on the fence, chomping an acorn like he was on a coffee break. Typical.

"Chuck!" I called up, urgency sharp in my voice. "What's going on? Why are they throwing everything away?!"

Chuck gave me a quick glance, then turned his face away like he was hiding how much it bothered him. “Humans,” he muttered, shrugging as if to deflect. “They throw their weight around. Just... don’t let it get under your fur. Go soak up some sun, Coop. Sleep it off.”

Nap it off?! Was he *serious*?? This was a *potential treasure* we're talking about!

But Chuck was already scampering away, leaving me alone to face destiny.

I turned back to the dumpster. Tail high, I crouched... *and leapt!*

Like a feline ninja, I landed inside, surrounded by mountains of forgotten oddities: battered books, mismatched socks, a half-deflated beach ball bobbing in the breeze.

I was in *heaven.*

This was my kingdom now.

Nosing around, I found a battered backpack—*perfect* for a cozy hideout—and wriggled my way inside. "Mmm," I murmured, inhaling the rich aroma of dusty adventures. "Smells like victory."

That’s when it happened.

CRASH!

A sudden racket behind me made every hair on my back stand straight up.

I whipped around—and there they were.

A gang of raccoons.

Bandits of the night. Marauders of the trash heap. And judging by their grins, *not* the friendly kind.

Gary, the biggest, squinted at me. "What’s a cat doing in our treasure trove?"

"Uh... inspection?" I stammered, puffing out my chest. "Quality control officer. Top of my class."

They exchanged suspicious looks, their masked faces twitching. The tallest one (fluffy enough to pass as a rogue cloud) twirled a polka-dotted sock between his paws. "What do you know about socks, kitty?" he asked.

I smirked.

Socks? Oh, please.

"Only that they make *fantastic capes,*" I declared, striking a heroic pose.

The raccoons froze. Then—*magic.*

Their eyes lit up like Christmas tree lights. One chubby raccoon let out a high-pitched cackle. "Capes! We could be superheroes!"

"THE POLKA-DOT PATROL!" someone shouted.

And just like that, it was settled.

Trash was no longer trash.

It was *fashion.*

It was *power*.

It was the beginning of a glorious new era.

Rocky (the tall one) started digging through the dumpster like a raccoon possessed. "I'll be the star model of 'Paw-some Patterns'!" he crowed.

Sneaky (the tiny hyper one) squeaked, "Dibs on the Hawaiian shirt! I'm gonna WORK it!"

And me? Oh, friends.

I was *the mastermind.*

"We'll start a collection," I proposed, my tail flicking with excitement. "We'll put on the greatest fashion show this neighborhood has ever seen—and then we'll raid the next dumpster together!"

Cheers erupted from the raccoons. High fives (and high paws) were exchanged. Plans were drawn in the dust. Dreams were born.

That afternoon, under the blazing sun and the watchful eyes of Chuck (who pretended not to care but was definitely *watching*), the Polka-Dot Patrol was officially formed.

A cat.

A pack of raccoons.

An unstoppable force of style and mischief.

And to think… it all started with a dumpster.

One cat's trash is another raccoon's treasure!

Hasta la vista, fashionistas! ✍🐾

MEOW OUT,

Cooper

Chapter 13: The Great Collar Rebellion: A Tale of Style, Strategy, and Subtle Dominance

Remember Covid? That stretch when the humans went full conspiracy, cleaning like it was a sport, having full conversations with their electronic boxes, and basically living inside. The world outside could wait; indoors was the new universe. That's when Mom, in a fit of either boredom or insanity, decided to introduce me to the *leash*.

Yes, a leash. On *me*, Cooper, the Sultan of the Sunbeam, the Master of the Staircase, the Feline of Freedom. Imagine! She clipped it on like it was no big deal and then opened the lanai door like *we* were going for a little trot around the neighborhood. I was horrified. I gave her my best wide-eyed stare of betrayal. Then I pancaked to the ground like a fluffy throw rug. *I do not walk on command and certainly not on a leash!*

But I haven't told you about the trick I learned shortly after that little misadventure.

Ah, yes... my first real *party trick*.

Back in the shelter—ugh, that place—it's a blurry, fishy-smelling memory now, with too many tails and not enough tuna. But I remember one thing clearly: the importance of *being noticed*. If you wanted a forever home, you had to *perform*. A flop here, a chirp there, a strategic purr—get the humans hooked, you know?

So, once I moved in with Mom and regained my throne (well, the chaise by the pool, but close enough), I decided to revive some of those long-forgotten skills.

Anyway, the humans there—well-meaning, of course—decided to accessorize me. And not in a good way. They slapped a black collar around my neck. Black. Plain. Functional. Not a single jewel, not even a pop of color. It looked like something you'd put on a street magician's rabbit. *Not* fit for a cat of my *stature*—yes, stature, because I sit like one. Regal. Unmoving. Magnificent.

But here's where it gets good.

That collar? One of those 'breakaway' gimmicks, sold as 'for our safety,' like I'd ever get myself tangled. Please. I've got this whole escape artistry thing down. But I wasn't about to wear that pedestrian strap of shame, so during the night—when the humans were gone and the shelter lights dimmed to a gloomy blue—I got to work.

It took me a few tries. At first, I pawed at it, rolled dramatically, and even tried wedging my head under the edge of the blanket. But then I found the trick. A little twist of the neck, a backwards stretch, a perfectly placed claw... *click*. That pathetic excuse for a collar *snapped right off*.

I stood there in the shadows, collarless, victorious, my fur unmarred by nylon. I strutted to the front of my cage and meowed—just once—a low, confident chirp to announce my triumph. The tabby in the next kennel looked at me with a mix of awe and confusion. "You're free?" he whispered.

"Damn right," I said with my eyes. Then I went back to sleep.

By morning, the humans were puzzled. "How did he get that off?" they muttered. They put it back on. *Amateurs*.

The next night? Same routine. Off it came. I made it look like it slipped off *by accident*, but we all knew better.

One morning, just as I was basking in the glow of another successful collar escape, a human worker—Janet, I believe her name was, with a voice like a squeaky toy and a fondness for wearing cat hair like it was part of her uniform—spotted me. Bare-necked. Glorious. Free.

She let out a frustrated sigh, the kind humans do when they realize they've been outwitted by someone with four legs and no opposable thumbs. "You *have* to keep it on during the day, Cooper," she muttered, fumbling with the limp collar in one hand and a clipboard in the other.

Apparently, it was "required." Required, can you believe it? She said something about how potential adopters—those wide-eyed humans who wandered through smelling faintly of hope and peanut butter—*needed* to see me wearing the collar. It made me "look available." *Available!* As if I were some common tchotchke on a shelf waiting to be scooped up during a clearance sale.

Let's pause here for a moment. I am not, nor have I ever been, merely *available*. I am *selective*. *Discerning*. I was not looking for just any human—I was waiting for *the right one*. Someone who understood that I required conversation, admiration, room-temperature pâté, and precisely 12 hours of uninterrupted lounging.

Still, they insisted. So each morning, Janet would march over with her defeated little sigh and reattach the black collar. I'd tolerate it just long enough to maintain appearances. I'd sit at the front of my enclosure, chest puffed, tail wrapped neatly around my paws, gazing through the glass with a look that said, "You wish."

Some days, people stopped. They'd coo. Tap the glass. Make kissy noises. Ugh. One woman even brought a small child who *screamed* at the sight of me. I recoiled, naturally. Who wouldn't? The child was wearing something sticky and smelled like sadness and apple juice. Not my crowd.

But I kept the collar on just long enough. Just until the crowds left, the lights dimmed, and the hush fell across the shelter once again. And then, like clockwork, I'd start the twist... the stretch... the flick... *click*.

By morning, Janet would find it on the floor of my enclosure, next to my food dish, like a polite "no thank you" note.

And so it went, day after day: their rules, my quiet rebellion.

You already know the story—the grand day I was adopted. The humans called it "Gotcha Day," as if they had somehow *caught* me. Cute. Let's be clear: I *allowed* myself to be selected. I scanned my options, sniffed the air, and when Mom and Dad walked in, I felt it. That rare, tingling certainty that these two might just be trainable.

They looked at me through the glass—Mom with that soft "ohhh" sound humans make when they're emotionally compromised, and Dad pretending like he wasn't already sold. I gave them The Look. You know the one. Chin slightly lifted, pupils dialed to "mysterious," tail wrapped just so. Regal. Intriguing. *Unmistakably Cooper*.

And just like that, I was out of the shelter, into a carrier that smelled like new car plastic and hope, and on my way to a place I would soon rule.

Now, for the first few weeks in my new kingdom—er, *home*—I behaved. Well, "behaved" in the sense that I let them think I was exactly what they wanted: sweet, compliant, ever-so-grateful. And yes, I even wore the dreaded black collar.

I played the long game.

I let them see me sitting near the window in it, looking angelic. I even purred when Mom scratched behind my ears while adjusting it. I could see the relief in her eyes—*he likes it!* Oh, poor dear.

But to her credit, Mom got the memo. One day, after a suspicious amount of internet scrolling and whispered conversation with Dad, she came home with something new.

A collar. But not just any collar.

This one... was blue. Deep ocean blue, with a hint of shimmer when the light hits it. Stylish, sleek, dignified. It brought out the exact shade of mystery in my eyes. *Now* we were getting somewhere.

She slipped it on with gentle hands and a hopeful smile. I allowed it, giving her a few grateful blinks and even a headbutt. You should've seen her beam. "Doesn't he look handsome?" she said to Dad, who agreed without even looking up from his newspaper. (Don't worry, I fixed that with a swift tail flick across his toast later.)

I wore the blue collar for weeks. It was... fine. Tolerable. Dashing, even. I looked in the mirror one day—yes, I do that—and thought, *Not bad, Cooper. Not bad at all.*

But of course, even the most regal accessory eventually becomes... ordinary.

And we cats, well, we do *not* do ordinary.

Ah yes, *the party trick*—my pièce de résistance, the ultimate display of feline finesse and subtle rebellion.

It had been weeks since my glorious adoption. I had explored every corner of the lanai, declared the couch my personal observation deck, and successfully convinced Mom and Dad that I preferred filtered water served in a ceramic bowl, not plastic, *never plastic*. All was going according to plan.

But then... the collar.

After my generous weeks-long act—wearing that fetching blue number like I was modeling for *GQ: Gentleman's Quarterly, Feline Edition*—I decided the time had come to introduce Mom to *the trick*. The same trick that flustered poor Janet back at the shelter. I had perfected it in the stillness of the night, like a stage magician preparing for his greatest illusion.

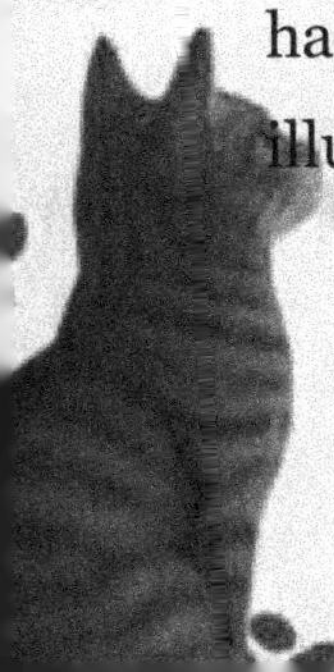

One crisp morning, after a satisfying nap by the sliding door, I performed the move. A graceful neck twist, a calculated shimmy, and—*click*—freedom. I padded over to the front door and laid the collar beside it. Not hidden. Not buried. *Placed.* As if to say, *"This is yours now. I'm done."*

When Mom found it, she gasped. "Cooper! How did this come off?" she said, like the collar had simply slipped away in the night on its own little adventure. She retrieved it and, with a loving but clueless smile, fastened it back around my neck. "There we go. All better."

Oh, sweet naïve woman.

I let her have her moment for one more day.

And then I did it again.

Same trick. Same collar. Same spot—right by the door. Like a gift. A polite *"No, thank you"* note once more.

The next morning? *Again.*

Five days in a row.

Every time, she'd find it resting exactly where I left it. At first, she thought maybe it was defective. "Is this too loose?" she muttered, examining the breakaway like it held some secret code.

By day four, I saw the change. That dawning realization in her eyes. That quiet moment when humans start to understand they are *not* in control.

And by day five?

She stood over me, collar in hand, then looked at me lounging regally on the windowsill, collarless, smug, absolutely unbothered. She sighed. "Okay, okay. No more collar."

Victory.

I didn't gloat. Not outwardly. I simply blinked once, slowly, as a king might acknowledge a subject who'd finally grasped the natural order of things.

From that day forward, my neck remained gloriously bare, my fur uninterrupted by nylon or bells or tiny dangling tags. And Mom? She finally understood: *I* decide what I wear. I may live in her house, but the rules? Well… they're negotiable, especially when you're me.

Remember—true power isn't loud. It's silent, smug, and usually covered in fur.

With supreme elegance and zero accessories, ✍🐾

MEOW OUT

Cooper

Chapter 14: The Great Boxspiracy

At first, I thought Dad and Mom were just doing one of their usual "tidy up the human space" things. You know, the kind where they move piles from one spot to another and act like they've done something important. I figured it was no big deal. I mean, humans are always bustling around, picking things up, putting things down, talking to themselves like anyone's listening.

Of course, the truth is...

I didn't really know *what* was going on.

Because I'm not allowed inside.

Yeah, you heard me.

Banned.

Prohibited.

Exiled from the Kingdom of Cushy Couches and Endless Napping Opportunities.

Apparently, it's because of my "hair situation." Something about my magnificent, luxurious fur shedding like soft, gray snowflakes all over Dad's sacred floors.

Hair everywhere? Please. I'm not shedding, I'm enhancing. Free interior design, no tip necessary.

Dad muttered something once about "not wanting to spend his entire life vacuuming cat hair," and from that moment on, I became an official member of the Outdoor Cat Club.

I mean, I'm not bitter. I have my sunny sidewalk kingdom, my bushes to hide in, my fence patrols.

Still... every now and then, when I see them inside, moving around with their clean socks and crumb-free snacks, a tiny, dignified sigh escapes my perfect little nose.

A cat can dream.

So when the giant, ugly dumpster appeared in my domain, and Dad started pacing like a chicken who lost his keys, I knew *something* big was happening.

But without access to the Indoor Secrets?

I was flying blind, friends.

Completely in the dark.

And that's when my whiskers tingled—the kind of tingle that said, *Cooper, a change is coming.*

I wasn't about to sit back and let this mystery unfold without me. No way. Not on my watch.

This calls for **action.**

Strategy.

Backup.

I padded over to the big oak tree at the edge of my kingdom and, with the authority of a general calling his troops to battle, I flicked my tail three times — the universal signal for an emergency meeting. (At least, that's what *I* decided it meant.)

One by one, my crew trickled in.

First came Sneaky — the wiry little raccoon with paws faster than lightning and a knack for finding snacks where no snacks should be. He skittered up, licking peanut butter off one paw and looking suspiciously innocent, which meant he'd been up to something delicious *without me.*

Next was Rocky — tall, fluffy, and so full of bravado he could barely fit through the bushes. Rocky always acted like he was the boss, but deep down, he knew who the real leader was. (Me, obviously.)

And then, after much dramatic sighing and acorn juggling, Chuck the squirrel sauntered in, still chewing like he had all the time in the world. *Typical Chuck.* I didn't exactly have high hopes for him — last time I asked him a question, he gave me advice that was basically just "go take a nap." (As if naps solve *everything.*)

They gathered around me, eyes gleaming with curiosity and maybe a little mischief, the sunlight filtering through the tree leaves and dappling our makeshift conference room in golden patches. It was perfect — dramatic, secretive, important. Just the way I like it.

I sat tall, my tail curling with importance. "Listen up, team," I began, my voice low and serious. "There's something *big* happening. Mom and Dad are tossing stuff into that giant metal monster like their lives depend on it. I don't know what it means yet, but it smells like opportunity... and mystery."

Sneaky leaned in, eyes wide. Rocky cracked his knuckles (or maybe that was just an acorn he crushed in his paw — hard to tell). Chuck yawned but stayed perched on the branch above, for once keeping his snarky comments to himself.

"I've heard humans say 'curiosity killed the cat,'" I said, puffing out my chest a little, "but not *this* cat." I narrowed my eyes, letting the gravity of the moment sink in. "Not today. Today, *we* are going to figure out what's going on."

A tiny breeze ruffled my whiskers as they all nodded solemnly — even Chuck, who looked like he was at least half-listening this time.

Operation Dumpster was officially underway.

After some intense staring, a bit of tail-flicking, and exactly three acorn tosses (thanks, Chuck), we finally decided on the obvious:

We needed a better view.

Not some half-baked, peek-around-the-bushes, squint-and-hope kind of look.

No.

We needed full, panoramic, crystal-clear surveillance of the inside of the house to figure out why they needed a dumpster.

I tapped a paw thoughtfully against my chin, my mind already racing. The humans were moving fast — boxes flying, bags piling up — and every second we wasted was a second closer to missing something *huge.* Like, what if they accidentally threw away a roast chicken? Or a feather pillow perfect for nesting? The stakes were higher than a bird on a power line.

Sneaky, naturally, wanted to climb straight up the side of the fence like a little raccoon ninja.

"I can scale it!" he declared proudly, flexing his tiny paws. "Easy peasy!"

Which would have been great... if he hadn't been chewing gum he found under a picnic table earlier and sticking to himself.

Rocky suggested we build a "lookout tower" out of the nearby trash cans. He even started stacking them, making a racket that could probably be heard three neighborhoods over.

(So much for *stealth mode.*)

Chuck, lounging lazily on a low branch, offered, "You could just climb a tree and *watch from above,* you know. Like a normal animal."

He said it with that casual squirrel smugness that made me want to flick a pinecone at his head.

Still... as much as it pained me to admit it, Chuck had a point. A higher view *was* smarter, faster, too.

I nodded thoughtfully, the sunlight glinting off my silky fur like I was some heroic explorer plotting the next great adventure. "We need elevation," I said, my voice full of leadership and destiny. "Height. Angle. Advantage."

The team looked up — the tall oak, the lower garden trellis, even the nearby neighbor's rusty fence. Potential launchpads everywhere, if you had the skill... which, of course, I did.

I paced in front of my team, my tail slicing through the air like a general inspecting his troops. "Here's the mission: Sneaky, you scale the left fence. Rocky, create a distraction if the humans look our way. Chuck... just... stay out of the way and try not to fall asleep mid-operation."

Chuck gave me a sarcastic salute with his tail, but I ignored him. Greatness requires ignoring small-minded critics.

The plan was simple.

Get high.

Get a view.

Figure out what in the name of all things crunchy was going on inside that giant, glorious house.

And then — after a lot of scrambling, sneaking, and more than one near-catastrophe (thanks, Rocky, knocking over a trash can) — we found it.

The perfect view.

From the crooked perch of the neighbor's old fence — a little wobbly, a little rusty, but *just* high enough — I could finally see inside.

I squinted through the bright afternoon light, my eyes narrowing into serious investigator slits. There, through the open garage door, I spotted them: **Mom and Dad.**

But not just *hanging out* or *cleaning a little.*

No.

They were in full human frenzy mode.

Mom's hair was tied up in a messy knot, strands sticking out like wild antennae, and she was taping boxes like her life depended on it.

Dad, meanwhile, was shuffling around, arms full of random stuff — books, lamps, picture frames, even a weird lamp shaped like a fish that I'd personally tried to destroy once (it was hideous).

Every few minutes, he would mutter something under his breath, glance at a clipboard, and stack another sealed box against the far wall.

Box after box after box.

Stacked like tiny little fortresses.

Row after row, building higher and higher, like they were preparing for battle.

I tilted my head, ears swiveling forward, trying to make sense of it.

What in the world was happening?

It wasn't just spring cleaning.

It wasn't the usual "let's move stuff around and pretend we're organized" show.

They were packing.

Really packing.

Taking things off shelves, wrapping them up in crinkly paper (which, by the way, looked like the most delightful toy if I wasn't so focused), and tucking them carefully into boxes. Then, sealing each one with big, noisy strips of tape that made me twitch every time they ripped through the air.

I glanced sideways at Sneaky, who was peeking around a garden gnome below. His mouth was hanging open, eyes wide.

Rocky, perched two feet over, was so still he looked like a statue, tail puffed out, paws clamped onto the fence.

Even Chuck, who normally had the attention span of a goldfish on espresso, had stopped chewing his acorn and was staring, wide-eyed.

"This..." I muttered, my voice barely a whisper, "This is big."

Questions whirled around inside my head faster than a feather in a hurricane.

Were they moving?

Were they getting rid of all the good stuff?

Were they *building a fortress to keep me out forever?!*

My heart thumped in my chest, a tiny, fierce drum of confusion and dread.

This wasn't just about a dumpster anymore.

This wasn't just about lost toys or hidden treasures.

Something was changing.

And whatever it was, it was way bigger than any of us realized.

My paws itched with excitement.

This wasn't just a mission anymore.

It was a *calling*.

Days passed, but the strange packing rituals didn't slow down. Every morning, I would find Mom and Dad elbow-deep in tape and bubble wrap, boxing up more and more of our life. Even my favorite sunbathing mat disappeared one day, folded and tucked into a box like it was nothing. I spent hours perched at my spy post, tail flicking anxiously, trying to piece it all together.

And then, just when the suspense was curling my whiskers into knots, **it happened.** A shiny, unfamiliar car rolled up to the curb one afternoon, its engine purring like a sleepy lion. I crouched low in the grass, every hair on my body standing at attention. A stranger stepped out — a tall woman with bright eyes, a giant smile, and shoes so clean they practically sparkled. She carried a folder stuffed with papers and kept glancing around, like she was sizing up *my* kingdom.

I slunk closer, my paws silent on the warm sidewalk. I ducked behind a flowerpot just in time to hear Mom's voice floating through the air.

"You're going to love your new home," she said, her voice warm and a little wobbly, like she was trying hard to sound cheerful.

New home?

My ears twitched so hard I almost lost my balance.

I pressed closer, every fiber of my being tuned into their conversation.

The woman nodded eagerly, her smile growing even bigger. Dad stood nearby, rubbing the back of his neck like he always did when he was nervous.

I felt my heart drop into my paws. *The mystery was solved.*

Clear as a bowl of fresh water on a sunny day.

We were moving.

The whole reason for the endless packing, the towering boxes, the swirling activity — it all clicked into place like the final piece of a jigsaw puzzle. I sat back on my haunches, dazed.

My sidewalk, my favorite sunny spot, the fence I used for secret missions, even the clover patch where I once buried an entire slice of pepperoni — *gone.*

We were leaving it all behind.

The weight of it hit me like a surprise splash from the garden hose.

Where would I nap now?

Where would I plot my grand adventures?

Would there be squirrels at the new place? Would the sun find me there?

What about my friends – would they be moving too?

For a long moment, I just sat there, whiskers drooping, tail lying still against the ground. The whole neighborhood buzzed around me — bees in the lavender, a dog barking two houses down, Chuck clattering noisily in a tree — but I heard none of it. My world had shifted under my paws.

Moving. It was happening for real.

And whether I liked it or not... I, Cooper the Crafty, was about to embark on the biggest adventure of my life.

Until next time, friends —

Stay curious, stay crafty, and never let a good sunbeam go to waste!

Meow for now,

Cooper

Chapter 15: Breaking Mews: We Moved

One day, Mom wandered onto my turf — the lanai — a sacred sun-soaked kingdom I patrol daily. She was talking to Dad about something she kept calling "the move." I stretched out on my favorite lounge chair, pretending not to listen, but every word floated over to me like a feather caught on the breeze.

"I hope he likes it there," she said, her voice full of that worried tone she uses when the food bowl is only half full.

"We don't have a screened-in lanai," she added, wringing her hands like she just realized the world might actually end.

"There are woods behind the new home... will he be safe?"

Safe? Woods? No screen? My ears perked up so hard I nearly flipped off the chair. Obviously, they were talking about *me*, Cooper, the most important resident of this household. Who else could inspire that level of panic? Certainly not Dad.

I gave my paw a few casual licks, playing it cool, but inside I was already making plans. A new kingdom to conquer? Woods to patrol? Screenless adventures? Oh, this was big.

Then came the shuffling — the suspicious kind that usually ends with someone (me) getting humiliated. And just like that, *ta-da* — the Cat Carrier of Doom materialized, like a bad magician's trick.

I stared at it in disbelief.

Really? This again?

I had *explicitly* instructed Rocky and Sneaky to dispose of that cursed contraption. I even offered bribes — the good treats, not the stale ones. But nooo, they probably got "distracted" by Chuck. Chuck, the furry acrobat who can't go five minutes without launching himself off the fence like he's auditioning for some kind of circus. Honestly, it's embarrassing how easily those two fall for his antics. One little backflip and — boom — critical mission: forgotten.

Amateurs.

I gave an exaggerated yawn and pretended not to care, but inside, I was plotting. Oh yes, *I was plotting*.

Mom, thinking she was the world's greatest actress, eased toward me with the Cat Carrier of Doom cradled in her arms like it was some sort of peace offering. She even had the nerve to smile sweetly, as if she were holding a bag full of treats and not a portable prison.

With the grace of a ballerina — or so she probably thought — she set it down in front of me and whispered my name like we were sharing a special secret.

"Cooper... come here, sweet boy..."

Oh, please. I wasn't born yesterday.

Now I had a real dilemma on my paws:

Option one — I could play along, stroll over, act innocent, and let them think they'd won.

Option two — I could stand my ground, puff up to twice my size, and show them exactly who they were messing with.

It was a tough call. On the one paw, surrender would be humiliating. On the other paw... well, standing my ground usually ended with me being stuffed into that carrier *anyway* — but with a lot more drama, hissing, and a few choice scratches for everyone involved.

Decisions, decisions.

Mom had been looking so tired lately — all that packing, organizing, muttering to herself about *"closing dates"* and *"change-of-address forms."* Honestly, it was exhausting just *watching* her. She needed a win. And, being the generous, selfless creature that I am, I decided to give her one.

I paused — dramatically, of course — locking eyes with her to make sure she *fully understood* the magnitude of the favor she was about to receive. Then, with a heavy, world-weary sigh, I casually hopped into the Cat Carrier of Doom, as if it were my favorite, most luxurious napping spot, like it was a first-class lounge reserved exclusively for Very Important Cats.

Mom gasped — in awe, I assumed — and quickly zipped the carrier shut before I could change my mind.

"Good boy, Cooper," she whispered, her voice cracking slightly like she might actually cry from the sheer wonder of my generosity.

I settled in, gave the side of the carrier a few impressive kneads for show, and then shot her a look that said, *"You're welcome."*

Honestly, if there were medals for acts of heroism during stressful human events, I deserved at least two.

The car ride, as expected, was nothing short of a *complete and utter nightmare.*

First, Dad tried to "secure" my carrier in the backseat like I was some kind of fragile cargo. Lots of fussing with straps and muttered curses. Honestly, it would have been faster if they'd just handed me the keys and let *me* drive.

Once we started moving, the indignities really kicked in. Every bump, every turn, every sudden stop had me sliding around like a loose meatball at the bottom of a spaghetti pot. And don't get me started on the air conditioning — one minute it was Arctic tundra, the next it was Sahara Desert.

I tried to maintain my dignity, of course. I sat perfectly still, eyes narrowed, emitting a low, steady *death glare* in Mom's direction through the carrier's bars. Occasionally, I let out a single, pitiful meow — not because I was scared, obviously, but because I wanted them to *feel bad.*

And they did. Oh, they did.

"Poor baby," Mom cooed from the front seat. *"Hang in there, Coop, almost there."*

Almost there? Ha. In cat time, this car ride had already lasted three eternities. I was going to need serious compensation after this ordeal — I'm talking extra treats, at least two new toys, and full bed privileges for a week.

At a minimum.

After what felt like a thousand years — give or take a century — the car finally came to a stop in a new neighborhood. I lifted my weary head and peered through the mesh of my carrier.

"This is it, Cooper," Mom said, turning around in her seat with a big, hopeful smile. *"This is your new home."*

I blinked at her, then turned my attention to the view outside. From my limited, imprisoned vantage point, things actually looked... promising. Very promising.

Wide, open yard — check.

Plenty of trees — check.

Birds fluttering around like feathered snack options — double check.

And — jackpot — a couple of squirrels doing whatever shady business squirrels are always up to.

I pressed my nose closer to the carrier window, my whiskers twitching. Maybe, *just maybe*, this wasn't going to be the worst thing that had ever happened to me. Of course, I wasn't going to let Mom know that *yet*. I had a reputation to maintain, after all.

Instead, I gave a long, skeptical blink and stayed perfectly still, as if weighing the pros and cons of this whole "new life" situation because a cat must remain *mysterious*, even when he's secretly plotting his first grand outdoor adventure.

And then — just when I thought I had the situation somewhat figured out — the strangest thing happened.

The big garage door groaned open, and Mom carried me — still imprisoned in the Cat Carrier of Doom — straight into the garage.

The garage.

Not the house.

Not the cozy new kingdom I had glimpsed from the car.

The garage.

I shot her a look through the mesh, one that clearly said, *Excuse me? This is not what we discussed.*

The door rumbled shut behind us, cutting off all escape. Then, in one swift motion, Mom unzipped the carrier and set me free in the garage.

"I just want you to get used to the house... the smells..." she explained in that soothing voice humans use when they're about to do something *completely unacceptable.*

I sat there for a moment, tail flicking, weighing my options.

On one paw, the garage smelled like an odd cocktail of old cardboard, paint cans, lawn equipment, and something suspiciously like Dad's forgotten sneakers.

On the other paw... it was big, and empty, and *new.*

I decided to be gracious. I did a slow, deliberate lap around the perimeter, sniffing every tire, every corner, every suspicious dark spot. The garage was... okay. Not exactly my dream palace, but acceptable for the time being. After all, a wise cat knows: before you rule a new kingdom, you must first *survey the territory.*

And if they thought this meant I'd *stay* in the garage for long, well — they clearly still had a lot to learn.

And just when I was starting to settle into my "temporary garage headquarters," it happened again.

Before I knew it, Mom had the Cat Carrier of Doom back out, sitting there in the middle of the floor like it hadn't just betrayed me mere hours ago.

Normally, this would've been the part where I bolted under the nearest pile of boxes and went full stealth mode.

But not this time.

Oh no — *this time,* I practically *ran* into the thing.

You see, I had important business to attend to. My friends back in the old hood — Rocky, Sneaky, Chuck the Showoff — they *needed* to hear about this new development. They needed a full report: the wide-open yard, the squirrel surveillance opportunities, the garage situation. This was *breaking news*, and I, Cooper the Great, was the only one qualified to deliver it.

I flung myself into the carrier with all the enthusiasm of a cat charging into an empty Amazon box. Mom looked stunned — clearly thinking she had finally "won."

She latched the door closed and murmured, *"Good boy, Cooper."*

Until the next adventure — Cooper, reporting live from the confines of the Cat Carrier of Doom, ready to uncover the secrets of my new kingdom. ✍✨

Meow Out, Cooper

Chapter 16: Sniff ya' Soon

I have now realized the move day was rapidly approaching. The telltale signs were everywhere: cardboard boxes multiplying like squirrels on espresso, Mom muttering to herself while wrapping everything in paper, and Dad walking around with a clipboard looking entirely too serious. I'd seen this pattern before. Something big was coming. And this time, I wasn't just supervising—I was going.

The gang knew it too.

Max, Rocky, and Chuck—my ride-or-die neighborhood crew—threw me a surprise goodbye party the night before The Big Box Migration.

It started casually. I was out doing my final perimeter check around the hedges when Max, the golden retriever with the permanent look of judgment, called out from behind the fence post.

"Hey, Cooper. Come with me."

When Max said that, it usually meant a showdown with the garden hose or waking up trapped in someone's garage. This time, though, something was different; there was a mischievous sparkle in his eye and a stolen stash of turkey slices dangling from his mouth. Naturally, I followed.

They'd set it up under the crepe myrtle tree—our usual hangout. A pizza box lid for a table, a puddle of hose water for drinks (Rocky insists it has "earthy notes"), and three catnip mice lined up like appetizers.

Chuck, the hyperactive squirrel, had made a banner out of a torn paper towel that read, *"Bon Voyage, Coop!"* It was misspelled. Obviously, but I appreciated the effort.

We ate, we chased shadows, we knocked over a lawn gnome just for tradition's sake.

And then—right there between a burp from Rocky and Chuck doing his usual backflips off the birdbath—it hit me.

I was leaving them.

I was really leaving them.

I'm not proud to admit it, but I got a little teary. Just a mistake. Like when the sprinklers hit your face at the wrong angle. Max saw me wipe my eye with my paw and

looked away like a gentleman. Chuck just said, "It's the catnip, bro," and gave me a quick nuzzle before pretending he had an itch.

I'd always pretended I was the lone wolf type. The cool cat. Aloof, untouchable. But those three—misfits, goofballs, furballs with zero sense of personal space—they were my crew.

Before we parted ways that night, Max gave me a final head bump and said, "Don't forget who you are."

"Yeah," Rocky added, "And if your new place has lizards, send pics."

Chuck just shouted, "FIGHT THE VACUUM!" and sprinted off into the bushes.

Classic.

The next morning, I climbed into my carrier, heart a little heavy but full of memories. As the car pulled away and my old turf disappeared in the rear window, I realized something important:

This wasn't the end. Just the beginning of the next chapter.

Still, I let out a long, theatrical sigh for effect. It's important to let the humans know you're grieving, even if you're lying on a plush blanket and nibbling on a freeze-dried salmon treat.

The ride was long. Too long. I gave a polite meow every ten minutes to remind them I was still back there. They responded with promises—"Almost there, Cooper!" and "You're going to love the new house!"—but I remained unconvinced. They also said the *Roomba* was harmless, and we all know how *that* turned out.

Eventually, the car slowed, turned down a street I didn't recognize, and stopped in front of a house that smelled... unfamiliar. No Max, no Chuck, no Rocky. No crepe myrtle tree. No pool. Just a wide front yard, some fluttery bushes, and—wait for it—an actual squirrel sitting *underneath the huge magnolia tree,* taunting me like I was the entertainment.

Oh, it was *on*.

They carried me around back and placed my carrier in the middle of the patio, which seemed so small compared to my previous kingdom. And then the door opened—and I stepped out, cautiously. One paw at a time, like royalty descending a grand staircase.

I sniffed everything. Patio furniture placement was all wrong. No scent markers, no known hiding spots, no ceiling perches. Yet.

The new backyard included some forest, which I immediately claimed as "Cooper's Wild Preserve"—and something Mom kept calling a *"pond."* Who was she kidding? It was clearly a drainage overflow. You can slap a fancy name on it, but if it quacks like runoff and smells like wet mulch, I'm not buying it.

Still, I'll admit... it had its charm.

This "pond" turned out to be the local hotspot for feathered freeloaders. The blue heron showed up first—tall, grumpy, and walking like he owned the place. I called him "Carl" until I got a better look. (Apologies, Carol.) Then came the ospreys—like hawks in designer sunglasses—swooping down with talons out, plucking fish from the muck with terrifying grace.

Quite the feeding frenzy. Honestly, it was better than cable.

I set up daily surveillance from the porch, front row seat, tail twitching like a metronome. It became my ritual: breakfast, patrol, bird-watching, nap. Repeat. Mom said I looked like I was "connecting with nature." I was actually plotting how to swipe a feather souvenir without getting dive-bombed.

Let's just say, I may not *like* water... but I do enjoy a good nature documentary—especially when I'm in it.

Maybe this place had potential.

Later that night, Mom brought out a box she hadn't unpacked yet and opened it just for me. Inside—my old blanket, my favorite green mouse, and a note taped to the top. In suspiciously sloppy handwriting, it read:

"Don't forget us.

—M, R & C"

Max. Rocky. Chuck.

I flopped onto the blanket and let out a satisfied purr. No, this wasn't the end.

It was a new kingdom. And I was ready to rule.

Still judging. But cautiously optimistic, ✍🐾

Meow Out 🐾

Cooper

P.S. I've already named the squirrel. His name is Gary. He's *asking*

Chapter 17: Air Traffic Chaos and Nap Zone Intrusions

Have I told you about any of my new friends?

No? Oh wow, you're in for a treat. Buckle up, buttercup.

So, first off, yes, we moved. It was traumatic. I had a routine. A sunbeam schedule. Preferred napping zones. And then BAM—boxes everywhere and humans getting sentimental over bubble wrap. Ridiculous.

But I digress.

Once we got to the new place, I had to rebuild my social circle. Street cred doesn't travel with you, apparently. But I'm nothing if not adaptable. (Okay, I'm also fabulous, but we don't have all day.)

Now, let me tell you about this *"pond."* My mom calls it that with a straight face, but let's be real—it's a drainage ditch. A glorified puddle with aspirations. Still, it's *my* puddle of dreams, and it happens to be the local hot spot.

Every evening, the air gets spicy with chirps and caws—my winged friends gather for what they call the *gaggle gathering*. It's like happy hour, but with feathers and questionable hygiene. The egrets are loud, the blue herons are dramatic, and the occasional osprey shows up fashionably late, like he's too good for us. (He is. He's majestic.)

I don't mingle much, mostly because I am a cat and they are potential snacks. But I do sit nearby, looking mysterious and aloof—basically doing quality control. Someone's gotta.

Oh! I *must* tell you—one of my favorite things about my winged friends (besides their unapologetic volume and general disregard for personal space) is how they approach "the pond." It's a whole *thing*.

Now, we've already established that the so-called "pond" is actually a glorified drainage ditch. But don't tell them that. They treat it like it's Lake Como. And the way they *land*? Pure drama. They use the stretch of grass between my house and the neighbors' like it's a runway at Bird Heathrow.

I'm serious. They come in low and fast, wings out like they're auditioning for Top Gun: Egret Edition. The honking starts mid-descent—clearly a group effort because no one wants to stick the landing without an audience. By the time they hit the water (or... mud), it's all splashes and feathers and triumphant flapping. You'd think they were Olympic divers.

I, of course, observe from my post on the lanai, occasionally offering a slow blink of approval. They need encouragement. Or judgment. Depends on the mood.

It's impressive, though. I admire the coordination. The flair. The absolute refusal to do anything quietly. It's inspiring, really. I mean, if you're going to arrive somewhere, make it known, right?

Anyway, the runway show happens daily, right around the golden hour. I call it *The Sunset Spectacular*. Tickets are free, and the squirrel (Gary, remember him?) is the usher, although he tends to forget halfway through and starts screaming at a stick.

So yeah—these birds, I swear, they put on a better show than anything on Animal Planet. Every day, like clockwork, they gear up for their runway descent into the Pond That Dreams of Being More. I sit perched in my observation tower (also known as "the back of the chaise"), paws tucked, tail flicking, looking like a fuzzy air traffic controller with no actual responsibilities.

The precision? Impeccable. The squawking? Excessive.

The vibes? *Immaculate.*

And don't even get me started on Carol. She's a blue heron with an attitude problem and a bright white streak that matches her energy. Carol does *not* wait for her turn on the runway. Oh no, Carol comes in sideways, flapping like she's late for a brunch reservation. I respect it.

The egrets, though—they're the *real* drama queens. Long necks, loud opinions, zero regard for air traffic rules. They circle three times like they're sizing up the pool at a party, then land with a splash that screams, "I'M HERE, DARLINGS."

Meanwhile, I remain poised, the silent audience to this feathery chaos. Occasionally, I make a little meow sound, just to let them know I *could* catch one... if I wasn't saving my energy for my mid-afternoon nap and second dinner.

Now, what truly completes this experience is Gary, the squirrel with an espresso problem. He's always darting around like someone wound him up too tight, half-burying

things, half-forgetting where he left them. Every time the birds land, Gary pops up like, "WHO GOES THERE?!" and then immediately forgets why he's yelling. The birds ignore him. I mostly do, too, unless I'm bored.

And listen—don't even get me started on the frogs.

They're like a barbershop quartet that got stuck in a rain barrel. They start their croaking around sundown, right when the bird show wraps up, like some kind of amphibian encore. You've got bass frogs, tenor frogs, and one overachiever who thinks he's a soloist. Their little choir loft is back behind the A/C unit, and let me tell you—it gets *loud*. But it's weirdly comforting. Like nature's white noise machine, if nature had a strong jazz influence and no volume control.

Did I mention my fabulous living space was not closed in?

Yeah. Shocking, I know.

Dad *keeps* telling me he's going to "enclose the lanai," whatever that means. I assume it involves magical walls, climate control, and a velvet chaise lounge for me. But as of now? Wide open. Just me, some furniture, a few play toys, and *every creature with a pulse* wandering in like it's an open house. No appointment necessary.

So naturally, I've taken it upon myself to **establish boundaries**. I'm out there daily, patrolling. Puffing my chest. Doing the slow catwalk perimeter check. I've left very clear messages in the form of glares, tail flicks, and the occasional guttural meow:

"This. Is. My. Space."

And for the most part, the locals respect it. Squirrels don't dare cross the line. Frogs know to keep their ribbits behind the bush. Even Gary—spazzy little acorn hoarder—gives me a wide berth. I am the undisputed ruler of the lanai.

But then… There was Carol the Heron.

Now, I know what you're thinking: "Wait, I thought Carol was a mallard?"

No, no. Different Carol. This one's taller. Like… stilt-walking supermodel tall. Long legs, long beak, major attitude. *The Heron.*

So there I am, mid-afternoon nap, deep in REM, probably dreaming about sashimi. I'm sprawled on *my* chair, the one with the faded floral cushion and the perfect amount of sunbeam. I'm totally zoned out—comatose, whiskers twitching, snoring softly like a tiny motorboat.

And then it happens.

I open one eye, as I do periodically (gotta stay alert, you know), and there. she. is.

Carol. The Heron.

Perched *on the arm of the chair next to mine.*

Staring down at me with those intense, prehistoric eyes.

Like she owns the place.

I didn't hear her land—which, let me tell you, is offensive. I'm a professional observer. Nothing gets past me. But she must have deployed some ninja-bird stealth mode, because I was *blindsided.*

We locked eyes. I didn't move. She didn't blink. It was a full standoff. A

moment so tense you could hear a pine needle drop.

I gave her the slowest, most deliberate head turn in feline history. A message loud and clear:

"Excuse me. Who invited you to my nap zone?"

She just stared. Tall. Unbothered. Like she *was* the HOA, and I'd violated a rule. The nerve.

And then... after what felt like an eternity, she gave a single low grunt (yes, herons grunt—it's unsettling), spread those massive wings, and lifted off like a pterodactyl at peace. No apology. No, thank you for the cushion. Just airlifted out of my personal space like she'd done *me* a favor by leaving.

I sat there in shock. Nap ruined. Ego bruised. But also? Kinda impressed.

Carol doesn't just take up space—she claims it.

We haven't spoken since. But the mutual respect is there.

She gets one free pass. One.

Next time? I'll be awake.

So yeah—life here's pretty lively for a "quiet" neighborhood. Drama in the sky, gossip in the pond, and me? I'm just here, paws crossed, looking fabulous and silently judging it all like the elegant neighborhood icon I am.

Alright, I hear the frogs warming up. Time to assume my post and prepare for the night shift. It's not easy being this glamorous and observant, but someone's gotta do it.

Till then, nap on and guard your furniture.

Meow out. 🐾

– Cooper 🐾

Chapter 18: Lawn and Order: Mole Victims Unit

The yard—my yard—is not just a patch of grass or a stretch of soil. It's my territory. My sanctuary. My green, sun-dappled kingdom. And I, Cooper the Crafty Cat, am its noble and vigilant guardian.

Or at least, I was... until they came.

I won't call them friends. They're not visitors or guests. They are invaders. Unwelcome. Unapologetic. And worst of all—stealthy.

Mikey the Mole and his entire subterranean empire moved in without warning. No knock at the door. No "hey, mind if we burrow under your begonias?" Not even a polite sniff. They just tunneled in like they owned the place.

At first, I was confused. There were signs—**suspicious signs**. Mysterious mounds of earth crop up overnight like fungal crop circles. Perfectly groomed grass pushed up in weird little humps, like tiny mole-made soufflés. The hydrangea bed looked like it had been attacked by a pastry chef with a vendetta.

Naturally, I blamed the usual suspects. The squirrels. (Always twitchy. Always suspicious. Was it Gary?) Then the rabbits. (Cute, yes, but deceptively chaotic.) For a brief moment, I even considered **gremlins**. It was that bad.

But no. This had **Mikey** written all over it.

Mikey the Mole—tiny, blind, and bold as brass. He and his minions had launched a full-scale underground campaign, complete with strategic tunnel systems and zero regard for lawn aesthetics. They were the gophers of guerrilla warfare. The trench-diggers of turf tyranny.

I could hear them at night—faint rustles beneath the soil, like whispers through the roots. The ground is shifting. The Earth breathing. My kingdom quakes from below.

He was smart. Too smart. Silent. Strategic. The kind of mole who could steal your backyard and your dignity before breakfast.

You'd almost admire him... *If he wasn't actively dismantling everything I held dear.* I now patrol with a new purpose. Every morning, I inspect the perimeter. Paws pressing lightly into the earth, tail twitching like a metronome of vengeance. I stare at the

fresh mounds with narrowed eyes, leaving long, deliberate sniffs—messages, warnings, **threats** in scent form.

The lawn? Cratered. The flower beds? Violated. My once-pristine nap spot under the hydrangea? A war zone.

And still, Dad didn't get it.

"Cooper! Stop digging! You're ruining the yard!"

Ruining it? *RUINING IT?!*

The outrage pulsed through my whiskers. My tail lashed like a furry whip of disbelief. I turned to face him—ears back, eyes wide with indignation, paws muddy but noble. I tried to explain. With my eyes. With my posture. With a series of sharply enunciated meows that clearly translated to:

"I'm not just rolling in dirt like some ordinary fluff—this is defense. I'm guarding the homeland."

But how do you tell your human that you're in the middle of a full-blown, subterranean siege? That the yard is no longer a gentle expanse of fescue and Florida weeds, but a **war zone**? That every mound of soil is a coded message from the enemy? That **this**—this claw-scrabble, tail-flicking chaos—isn't mischief?

It's a battle**.**

And Mikey the Mole?

He's not just some blind, bumbling ground-pest. No. He is enemy number one. A tunneling tyrant. A dirt-dwelling disruptor. The Napoleon of the netherworld. Every time I filled in one of his tunnels with strategic paw-stomps and dirt kicks, two more sprouted up overnight, taunting me. Mocking me. Like he had blueprints. Like he was playing chess, and I was in check.

Every fresh pile of earth was a slap in the face. A calling card. A declaration of war signed in loam and audacity.

He was a shadow beneath the gardenias. A soft-footed saboteur who moved like smoke and laughed like thunder—*if thunder squeaked and smelled faintly of worm breath.*

And me?

I was just one cat. One noble soul. Armed only with a plastic shovel (liberated from the neighbor kid's sandbox), a heart full of righteous fury, and legs so grass-stained they looked camouflaged. My fur held traces of mulch and defiance. My claws were worn from patrol duty. My naps? Shorter. Shallower. Tense.

Because I knew *he was still out there.*

I was no longer lounging in the lap of domestic luxury. I was a soldier. A sentinel. A muddy-pawed freedom fighter determined to win back his kingdom.

And if Dad didn't understand now?

He would.

Someday, when the mounds stop rising... when peace returns to the begonias... when the yard is mine again and the last mole tunnel is silent...

But I wasn't giving up.

I dug trenches. I built decoy tunnels. I staged elaborate dirt traps behind the rose bushes. I even attempted psychological warfare—staring menacingly into the mole holes for hours, unblinking, whispering, *"I know what you did."*

And still... he came.

The sun scorched my back. My paws ached. My tail twitched with frustration. Hope was slipping, like litter off a clean tile floor.

And so, in my lowest moment, I did what any fearless feline pushed to the brink would do:

I peed.

Not out of desperation. Out of strategy. Precision. Purpose. The kind of primal message no mole could ignore.

I marked every tunnel. Every path. Every fresh pile of soil was anointed with the unmistakable, non-negotiable scent of *ownership*.

By the hydrangeas. Behind the tree. Right next to that smug garden gnome who never lifts a finger but always looks so superior.

And guess what?

It worked.

The next morning: silence. No new hills. No fresh trails. The yard was still. Glorious. Victorious.

I strutted across my reclaimed kingdom, tail raised in triumph, the morning sun catching my whiskers like golden rays of glory. I gave the hydrangeas a celebratory sniff. I even gave the gnome a respectful nod. He nodded back. (In my head, at least.)

Dad still doesn't get it. He muttered something about "behavioral issues" and "cat therapy."

Mom's furious about the pee.

But I don't care.

Because I know what I did, and somewhere, deep beneath the earth, *Mikey* knows it too.

You don't mess with Cooper the Cat.

Not in my yard. Not on my watch.

Mole Patrol: Mission accomplished.

Until next time, keep your paws clean, your tail high, and your tunnels mole-free.

This is Cooper the Crafty Cat—guardian of the green, defender of the dirt, and undefeated champion of the backyard battleground—signing off.

Stay sharp. Stay fierce. Stay fabulous.✍🐾

Meow Out 🐾

Cooper

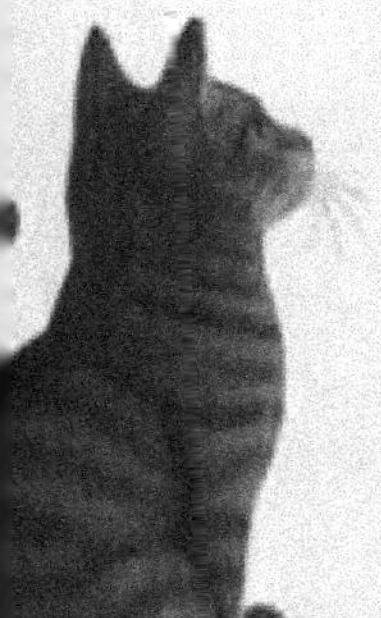

Chapter 19: Escape from Cat Camp: The Cooper Chronicles

I told you the story about staying at the vet and my daring escape from the exam room. And of course, I am no longer welcome back there. Apparently, when you open a cabinet, scale a wall, and open doors, people *remember* you.

This, understandably, caused quite a ruckus in our household. Mom was beside herself. "Who's going to take care of Cooper when we travel?" she cried, eyes wide, like I might erupt into chaos at any second. (Alright, sure, call me unpredictable. It's part of the charm.)

She tried several options. The first one? A *new* vet. She thought she was being clever. New location. New people. Fresh reputation.

Wrong.

This place had the nerve to put me in a "cat condo." Sounds glamorous, right? You'd think velvet cushions, tuna on tap, and a view of a koi pond.

Nope.

It was a glorified storage cube with bars. A two-level box with a plastic shelf and a towel that smelled like a mop. "Luxury," they called it. I've seen better accommodations inside shoe boxes.

To make it worse, they had *other cats* in similar "condos," staring at me like I was the new inmate. One of them hissed at me from across the hall—I hissed back, naturally. The standoff lasted hours. That's when I realized... this wasn't a vacation. This was jail.

I didn't eat on the first day. Out of protest, obviously. On the second day, I made it my mission to escape. Again.

Unfortunately, the doors here had *locks,* and the staff had clearly been briefed on my "history." I heard one of them refer to me as "the Houdini Tabby." A compliment, really, but it meant they were watching me like hawks. Or worse—like ospreys from the pond.

When Mom came to pick me up, I didn't even try to hide my disgust. I turned my back when she opened the carrier. Not out of spite—okay, maybe a little—but because I wanted her to *see* what her betrayal had done. She cried, "Oh, Cooper, I missed you!" and tried to smother me in kisses.

I tolerated exactly 3.5 seconds.

At home, I sulked under the patio couch for the better part of the afternoon, just to drive the point home. I knew she felt guilty. She offered treats. I took them, begrudgingly. Let's not be dramatic.

That was the last time she tried the cat condo.

We were back to the same spot: no one to take care of me.

Mom stood on the lanai with that worried look on her face again, staring at her phone like it might magically produce a solution. Dad tried to act like he wasn't involved, but I saw him slowly back out of the room like a man who just remembered he had "important yard work" to do.

Now, let's be clear—I don't need *much* care.

Some lobster mac and cheese. A little cream in a crystal dish (not that ceramic nonsense). Four belly rubs a day—no more, no less. I'm low-maintenance, really, just with standards.

You'd think this wouldn't be so hard. But apparently, my "reputation" had gotten around. Word travels fast in the cat care community. I overheard Mom on the phone trying to convince someone I had "matured." Ha! I'm an icon. Icons don't *mature,* we evolve.

She even made a list titled "*Cooper's Routine*" that read more like a treaty negotiation.

- 6:00 a.m. – Breakfast (only eats if food is plated right)
- 9:00 a.m. – Nap (sunbeam preferred)
- Noon – Tail chase or existential staring
- Afternoon – Optional treat, belly rub (on his terms)
- Dinner – Lobster mac and cheese (warmed, obviously)

She posted it on the fridge with a magnet that says *"Live, Laugh, Meow."* Honestly, humiliating.

In the end, she said, "Cooper, if we can't find anyone to stay with you, we might have to *take you with us.*"

I stared at her. Hard. Like, *burning a hole through your soul* hard.

We both knew what that meant.

The *carrier.*

The *car.*

The *destination unknown.*

And possibly… another cat condo.

So yeah, I've started buttering up the neighbors. Literally, I left a stick of butter on their doorstep in a show of goodwill. If that doesn't work, I'll sit on their porch and yowl until they cave. Someone around here has to recognize greatness when they see it.

Mom came running up to me one day, eyes sparkling, hair slightly frazzled (as usual). She crouched down, put her face inches from mine, and whispered like we were planning a bank heist.

"I have a *super* idea," she said, all breathy and excited. "The neighborhood *kids* can take care of you!"

I blinked.

Once.

Then twice, slower this time, to make sure she saw the full weight of my disbelief.

The *kids?* As in, the sticky-fingered, loud, chaos agents who once tried to ride Chuck like a pony and put sunglasses on a lizard? *Those* kids?

"They're responsible," she insisted. "And they *love* animals!"

Yes. *Too* much. In that aggressive, over-hugging, let's-play-dress-up way. Love like that leaves trauma.

Despite my better judgment, I agreed to a supervised test visit. I'm not unreasonable. Just vigilant.

The first one to arrive was named Maddie. She was about eight, wore mismatched socks, and had a glittery notebook labeled "Cooper's Daily Journal." Cute. Dangerous. She immediately asked, "Can I give him a makeover?" To which Mom, thankfully, said no. I made a note to avoid eye contact moving forward.

Then came her younger brother, Tyler. Tyler introduced himself by shouting "COOOOOPER!!" and flinging a feather wand directly at my face. I did not flinch. I did not move. I simply turned and walked away like a professional.

Over the next hour, they followed me around with a clipboard, a measuring tape, and a suspicious amount of enthusiasm. They tried to brush me (not my approved brush), offered me a goldfish cracker (inedible), and made up a theme song for me on the spot. It was... catchy, but undignified.

By the time Mom came back to check in, I was perched on the very top of the couch, out of reach, staring down like a disapproving landlord.

"Well?" she asked, hopefully.

I sighed.

Look, I'm not saying the kids are *terrible*. They're just... very *kid*. Loud. Unpredictable. Always sticky. But they meant well, and I'll admit—Tyler did refill my water with crushed ice. That earned him one slow blink of approval.

So, am I ready to endorse them as official caretakers?

Let's just say: probationary status. Under review. Daily evaluations to be conducted.

I am, after all, a professional.

Mom and Dad left shortly after that, blowing kisses, promising they'd "be back soon," and acting like they were sending me off to summer camp. Please. This was no camp. This was a full-blown *experiment in survival.*

I was left with the kids.

Let's just say... the arrangement lasted a whopping *day*.

By mid-morning, Tyler had tried to build me a "cat obstacle course" using couch cushions and spaghetti noodles. Maddie attempted to brush my tail into a heart shape. There was talk of a TikTok video. I knew I had to act fast.

That evening, under the cover of fading sunlight and the noise of a bubble machine malfunctioning on the lanai, I made my move.

I reached out to *Carol and Gary* —my trusted associates and longtime allies in the neighborhood underground. Carol, the blue heron with eyes like polished obsidian and a resting glare that scares raccoons. Gerard is a squirrel with the strength of a bulldozer and the grace of a falling bookshelf. Together, they're the kind of crew you want when you're planning a break in the woods.

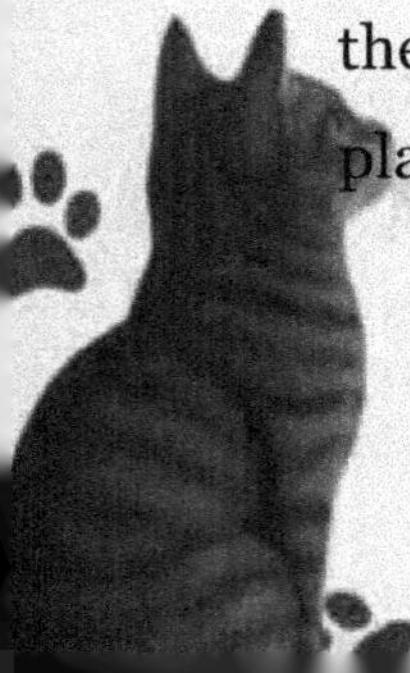

At precisely 7:08 p.m., I gave the signal (three tail flicks and a fake yawn), and they appeared at the drinking pond like shadows in the dusk. Carol had already cased the area. Gary brought snacks—dry food from the Davis' porch and half a stolen mozzarella stick.

Without a word, we slipped through the woods and into the darkened path between the trees. Freedom.

They led me deep into the woods, where the trees swallow sound and no glitter stickers or macaroni crafts can find you. It was quiet. Peaceful. Slightly damp. We hunkered down under an overturned canoe someone had abandoned long ago, a known feline safehouse. Carol paced. Gary snored. I stared out at the moonlit pond (okay, drainage ditch) and let out a long, satisfied sigh.

I was safe.

And more importantly, I was in control.

No stickers. No obstacle courses. No heart-shaped tails. Just me, my crew, and the crisp scent of pine needles and defiance.

Of course, I had no idea what tomorrow would bring. But I'd rather take my chances with coyotes than get filmed for TikTok in a bowtie again.

Every morning, just as the sun cracked over the tops of the pines and the dew made my whiskers tingle, we ventured to the edge of the woods.

Carol was always the first to arrive—silent, graceful, dramatic as ever. Gary followed, lumbering through leaves like a furry freight train. And then there was I. Cooper. Noble. Watchful. A little hungry.

We perched together on the ridge near the hollow log, just above the backyards where lawn sprinklers hissed and bird feeders swayed like baited traps. From there, I could see our house—my house—standing quietly. It looked... empty. Too quiet.

I scanned the windows, every curtain, every flicker of movement. Every morning. Hoping.

Hoping she returned.

Mom.

She wasn't perfect, I'll say that. She left me with children who once tried to feed me a crayon and called it "medicine." But she also knew the exact way to scratch behind my ears, so my back foot twitched. She turned on my heating blanket when the weather dipped. She whispered secrets to me like I was more than a cat... like I was family.

And now she was gone. Off who-knows-where with Dad, probably somewhere with no cell signal and too many decorative pillows.

Gary tried to cheer me up by chasing a squirrel and immediately falling into a puddle. Carol brought me a lizard—half of one, anyway—which I politely declined. It wasn't the same.

Still, we returned every morning.

Waiting.

Watching.

Wishing for the sound of her car. The creak of the front steps. That unmistakable call: "Coooooper?"

But until then, I remained in the woods. A sentinel. A shadow. A cat with a plan... and a little bit of hope.

It seemed like *forever,* but the day finally arrived.

Mom came home.

I heard the sound first—a low hum, like the purr of a tired but determined beast—and then the crunch of tires on the gravel. I was at the edge of the woods in a flash, ears forward, eyes locked on the driveway. Gerard didn't even have time to finish his pinecone snack. Carol hissed at a squirrel and bolted into the underbrush, sensing the shift in energy.

The car door opened. A figure stepped out.

It was her.

Hair slightly windblown, suitcase in one hand, phone in the other, calling out, "Cooper? Coooooper?"

And just like that, the steel wall around my heart cracked.

I didn't run, mind you. I'm not a dog. There was no dramatic sprint or open-pawed leap. But I *walked* out of those woods like a legend returning from exile. Head high. Tail tall. Dignity intact—but barely.

She saw me and dropped her bag.

"Oh my *Cooper!*" she cried, arms flung wide.

I stopped three feet short. Looked her up and down. Blinked twice. Then, slowly, cautiously, I closed the distance and leaned against her legs. Just a touch. Just enough.

She scooped me up and smothered me in kisses. I allowed it—for about eight seconds.

Then I wriggled free and strutted inside, like *maybe* I hadn't been living under a canoe with Gerard for a week, like I wasn't covered in a fine layer of leaf bits and secrets. Like I belonged there.

Because I did.

Everything smelled like home again—clean towels on my favorite couch, my toys neatly placed where I had left them.

Mom made me a bowl of cream.

I sat on the couch as the sun streamed in, finally back in my rightful place as Ruler of All I Survey.

And as for the kids?

Let's just say there's a new rule: no more glitter near the cat.

Back on the throne. No autographs, please. ✍🐾

Meow Out 🐾

Cooper

Chapter 20: Peck of Respect

Ah, yes, the evening *Gaggle Gathering* at the glorified "pond." (Ahem, let's be honest—it's a glorified drainage ditch with delusions of grandeur.)

Now, allow me—Cooper the Crafty Cat, feline observer extraordinaire—to paint you a picture as the sun begins its dramatic descent (as if auditioning for a soap opera), a rather dignified lineup forms at the edge of the water.

There's Carol the Heron—tall, silent, slightly judgy. She always arrives first, like she's the one who made the reservation. She tiptoes through the shallows like she's royalty, trying not to scuff her suede shoes. She positions herself just so, neck extended in that "I'm listening but also above all of this" posture.

Next come the ospreys—a whole family of them. Loud, flappy, and entirely without boundaries. They land like clumsy penguins on a slippery slide. One always skims the water a little too close and pretends it was "on purpose." They bring snacks, mostly fish, which they eat loudly with eye contact. It's a lot.

And then, like always, it's time for the Great Toe Dip. Every single one of them—even Carol—tiptoes up to the edge and sticks just the tiniest bit of toe in the water, like they're expecting it to explode or turn them into frogs. Then they all freeze and stare out at the water like it's giving out free snacks.

Do they chat? Oh yes. Gossip flows like pond scum in the wind. Carol murmurs about the ducklings who think they own the place. The ospreys roll their eyes at that one squirrel who's been "training for a triathlon" by splashing through their territory. And everyone agrees that the turtles are just *too* smug.

I, of course, remain above it all, watching from my strategic perch (also known as the green and white chaise (Mom believes that is her chair, but I just let her sit in it every once in a while, which I've claimed as my throne). I do not mingle. I observe. I judge. I nap.

One evening, just as I was settling in for my third nap of the evening (which follows my post-dinner pre-bedtime snooze), I was sprawled luxuriously on the sun-warmed slate of the back terrace, tail curled just so, paws folded under my chest like a sphinx who's seen too much. The golden hour was draping itself lazily over the yard, painting everything in soft honey tones and long, dramatic shadows. The pond—*pardon me,* the

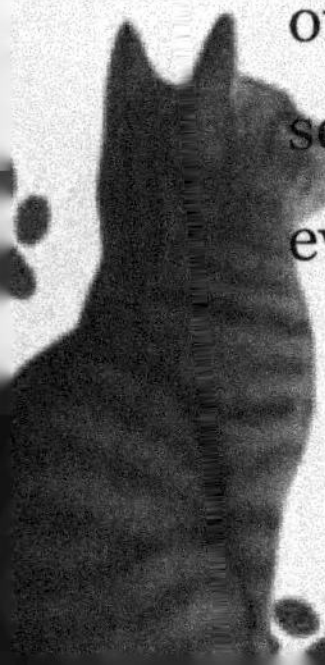

glorified puddle with dreams—was unusually still, reflecting the pink-tinged sky like it thought it was Monet's muse.

And just as I was about to slide into that delicious in-between place where dreams of tuna and catnip toys await—*whoosh.*

Something shifted. Not the wind. No, this was sharper, sleeker. A ripple in the sky itself.

Harry the Hawk.

He was gliding low, far too low for it to be casual. Not a flap, not a sound—just a shadow stretching across the grass like a warning whispered in feathered Morse code. His wings carved the air with all the grace of a ballet dancer and all the intent of a dive bomber. He wasn't flying *over* the pond. Oh no. He was skimming it. Shaving the surface so closely, his reflection looked nervous.

Harry and I—we have history. He's pulled this stunt before. Comes in low, scanning the scene like he owns the place, only to catch sight of *me*. And when he does? He bails. Every time. Doesn't flap. Doesn't falter. Just shifts his trajectory ever-so-slightly and disappears into the treetops like some high-altitude illusionist.

It's always the same look. That brief flick of his head mid-glide. The locked-on stare. Cold. Calculating. And then—just like that—gone.

And there I was, left with my fur puffed by the sheer arrogance of his wingspan, blinking that deliberate, smug stare only a cat can pull off, because I knew exactly what it meant: *Not today, Cooper.*

That evening was no different. As he slid past, his eyes—those laser-focused amber marbles—locked with mine. For half a heartbeat, we existed in the same moment. Predator to predator. Top of the food chain to... other top of the food chain. I didn't flinch. I didn't blink. I just watched him the way a king watches a visiting dignitary who forgot to bow.

And as expected, he peeled off toward the oaks, his silhouette melting into the dusk, leaving only a slight shiver in the reeds and a stunned silence among the bird council gathered at the water's edge.

Carol the Heron looked rattled. One of the ospreys dropped its fish.

I didn't move. Didn't need to. I simply tucked my head under one paw and resumed my rightful slumber. Because in this yard, over this glorified pond, only one of us rules the twilight.

And it's not Harry.

Carol the Heron, with her long legs like a supermodel crossed with a pair of chopsticks, climbed out of the pond looking like she'd just seen her entire life flash before her beak. Her feathers were fluffed in all the wrong directions, her usual sleek silhouette now resembling a thrift-store feather boa that had been through a leaf blower.

She was *shaking*, mind you—not mildly, not daintily, but full-on twitching like Gary the Squirrel on one of his infamous espresso benders. (You remember Gary. Poor nutcase. One acorn short of a picnic and absolutely no business near a coffee bean. Last week, he ran full speed into the side of the compost bin and claimed he saw the face of Elvis in a rotting banana peel.)

Anyway, back to Carol. She wobbled out of the water with all the grace of a soggy marionette, knees bending the wrong way like nature had second thoughts halfway through assembling her. She paused at the edge of the lawn, took one long breath—probably counting to ten in her head—and then began her slow, deliberate walk toward the lanai.

Now, you must understand: Carol does *not* do social calls. She is a bird of quiet superiority, a still-life painting come to life. But tonight? Oh no. Tonight, she was a quivering wreck in need of emotional triage.

She stepped onto the lanai, her giant feet clicking gently on the tiles, neck still half-tucked like she wasn't sure whether to stay upright or curl into a feathered ball. I blinked slowly from my perch on the chair cushion (embroidered, might I add, with an unfortunate pineapple motif—*humans*), and tilted my head ever so slightly to acknowledge her presence. Regal. Aloof. Perfect.

Then—*and I swear on my secret stash of catnip mice*—Carol leaned down. Slowly. So slowly, I thought maybe she was malfunctioning. And with the delicacy of a diplomat offering peace, she gave me... a peck, right on top of my head.

A quick, feathery bop. Barely there. But deliberate. A thank-you? A blessing? A nervous tic? Who's to say?

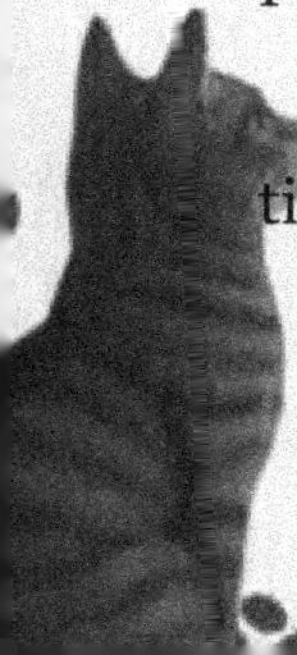

And then she stood back up, taller, calmer, perhaps a touch less electrified, and tiptoed off with what remained of her dignity.

I didn't move. I simply flicked an ear and returned to my loaf position, absorbing the gravity of the moment.

Because when the queen of the pond kisses the guardian of the pond?

You let it happen.

And then you nap.

Until the next twilight tale,

Meow out. 🐾

– Cooper 🐾

Chapter 21: Mission Impawsible

Did I mention that I live on the lanai? Oh, excuse me—let me introduce myself properly. I'm Cooper the Crafty Cat, ruler of the lanai, master of the mid-morning nap, and undisputed king of the chaise lounge.

Yes, it's been ten whole years, and my mom and dad *still* don't let me inside to snuggle on their bed. Outrageous, right? But hey, I make the most of my outdoor paradise. The lanai is my domain, and I've made it *just right* for a refined feline like myself.

I've got all the essentials: a long, luxurious chaise where I can stretch out and sunbathe like the royalty I am. My meals? Only the best. Lobster treats are my favorite—call me fancy, I don't care. And then there's my trusty scratching pole. I keep these claws sharp and ready for action, just in case a bold lizard or an overly curious bird decides to test my authority.

Sure, I dream of the forbidden land beyond the sliding door—where the blankets are fluffier and the pillows smell like mom—but for now, I reign supreme on the lanai. It's my palace, my perch, my paradise.

And if you hear a sudden sprint followed by a tumble into a potted plant? Don't worry. That's just me, Cooper the Crafty Cat, doing my thing.

So one day, I got a crazy idea—which makes sense, because, well, I *am* Cooper the Crafty Cat, after all. And what's life without a little drama and adventure?

I figured, if I could just get onto the *roof*, then maybe—*just maybe*—Mom would finally let me in through a window. A grand entrance! A bold move! My golden ticket into the forbidden kingdom of fluffy beds and forbidden snacks.

Now, let me be clear: this wasn't some impulsive, zoomie-fueled leap. Oh no. My home is *two stories* tall, so this required real strategy. I began with a full reconnaissance mission, pacing the lanai and observing every tree and branch that dared come close to the house. I took notes. I ran simulations (a.k.a. pacing in circles and twitching my tail). I analyzed wind speed and bark texture.

And I wasn't alone. I consulted my old pal Sammy the Squirrel, rooftop acrobat extraordinaire. Sammy's been running the eaves for years and knows every angle, every slip-point, and every good sunning spot. I met him at our usual spot near the hibiscus bush and laid out my plan. He chattered excitedly—probably impressed by my daring spirit (or maybe just distracted by a peanut, hard to tell with Sammy).

Together, we mapped the route: branch to the grand roof. It was bold. It was brilliant. It was crafty.

Just the way I like it.

I picked the *perfect* day for my big rooftop mission. The skies were clear, the breeze was light, and most importantly, Mom let me *out* of the lanai that morning. Freedom. Sweet, sweet freedom.

I hung back at first, lounging casually like I didn't have a master plan brewing. But don't be fooled—inside, I was all systems go. I waited patiently, just long enough to confirm that both Mom and Dad were staying home. After all, what good is a daring rooftop leap if there's no audience to witness your greatness?

Then it was time. Operation Rooftop was officially underway.

I sprinted toward *The Tree*. You know the one—it leans just enough, and its limbs reach toward the roof like nature's personal cat ladder. I launched myself up the trunk in a blur of fur and focus. Up, up, up I climbed, muscles coiled like springs. And then...

I *flew*.

Through the air, over the gardenias, paws outstretched like a feline superhero. My only regret? My parents didn't see it. Not a single second. I mean—seriously! I bet I was more impressive than Superman. He wears a cape. I *am* the cape.

I landed on the roof like a whisper. Not even a tile rattled. Just me, Cooper the Crazy Cat, surveying my kingdom from above.

Oh, I was *so* excited and absolutely *pleased* with myself. I *did it*! My plan was working flawlessly. I was on the roof—*on the actual roof*—and now it was time for the final piece: getting Mom and Dad's attention. The grand finale.

I dashed across the sun-warmed shingles with the grace of a feline Olympian—no hesitation, no slip, just pure, four-pawed precision. Below me, the world looked small and foolish, especially the screened lanai, which, I should mention, Dad *finally* got around to enclosing. About time, really—my architectural advice had gone ignored for months.

From my elevated stage, I struck a pose worthy of a marble statue and unleashed a meow—no, a *yowl*—that echoed through the neighborhood like a feline battle cry. It was my mighty rooftop roar, a proclamation to birds, squirrels, raccoons, and any nosy neighbor within earshot: **The King is above, and he is hungry.**

Mom heard me. Of *course* she did. I knew she would. And oh, her reaction did *not* disappoint. She stepped outside, looked up, and *gasped.* A proper, hands-on-face, jaw-dropping gasp.

"JIM!" she yelled (that's Dad, in case you're wondering). He came out, looking wildly confused, as if a flying cat on the roof was the last thing he expected that day. I mean, really? *I* wasn't confused. I had a plan.

Then came the moment that made my whiskers twitch with disbelief—Mom told Dad to get the ladder.

The ladder! As if I would *ever* climb into Dad's arms *twenty feet off the ground*. Please. I have standards. And claws.

Meanwhile, I'm trying to *tell* them—clearly, loudly, with very well-enunciated meows—that there's a perfectly fine window right there on the second floor. But they were too busy clanking around with the ladder and yelling things like, "Don't fall!" and "Put the ladder here?"

Eventually, poor Dad was exhausted from lugging around what looked like a 50-pound medieval siege weapon. Mom sighed, waved him off, and said, "Forget it. He'll figure it out." She turned to go back inside, on her way to her office, *which, I should mention*, is on the second floor, with a window.

She sat down at her desk like she had *already forgotten* about me. Unbelievable.

But then, I knocked. Just a soft tap on the glass. Tap-tap. Her head snapped up.

She saw me. She *yelped* with joy. And *finally—finally*—she opened the window. And guess what?

I, Cooper the Crafty Cat, **gained access to the house through the window!**

Victory. Sweet, glorious victory. I strutted in like I owned the place (because let's face it—I kinda do), tail high, eyes gleaming. Ten years on the lanai, and now... sweet indoor territory.

Just as I was savoring my sweet, victorious entry—my first steps into the mysterious *indoor world*—Mom tried to scoop me up.

Excuse me?

That was *not* part of the plan. I didn't climb a tree, soar like a superhero, and mastermind an operation with Sammy the Squirrel just to be *carried back out* like some rogue raccoon. Oh no.

So, I did what any self-respecting feline would do: I stretched long, turned sideways, wiggled like a slippery noodle, and made myself *impossibly* difficult to hold. After a few seconds of struggle, Mom sighed and put me down.

Yes. Victory, part two.

She seemed to give up—not out of defeat, but out of sheer exhaustion. I could tell the morning's rooftop drama had taken its toll. She just watched me with that "I can't believe this cat" look as I wandered off, tail high, paws soft against the cool indoor floor.

And wander I did.

Room by room, I began my inspection. Comparing textures, vibes, smells. The couch? Plush, but not as sun-warmed as my chaise. The kitchen? Intriguing... lots of mystery smells. Possibly cheese. The hallway runner? Excellent for zoomies. The upstairs carpet? Not bad. Soft, springy—like a cloud under a paw.

I stopped by the laundry basket, sniffed a pair of Dad's socks, and made a mental note: potential toy.

Every space had a story, every nook a new secret. I was like an explorer in a strange new land. My land. And I had *earned* this tour.

I continued my grand tour with the grace of a diplomat and the curiosity of, well... a cat who had just broken a ten-year barrier.

The hallway led me to the most sacred, most whispered-about place in all my years of dreaming—the bedroom. *The bed.* The Holy Grail of fluff. The cloud of legends. I crept in, slowly, reverently. The room was quiet, sun filtering in through the curtains just so. And there it was.

Their bed.

I approached it like a lion stalking prey. Except instead of pouncing, I hopped up like it was no big deal (even though inside I was screaming with joy). I turned around a few times, giving the cover a test knead. Oh yes. This was *it*. I nestled right in the center where the pillows meet—the perfect divot—and let out a content sigh.

After all these years, the rumors were true. The bed was *amazing*.

I stretched luxuriously, paws reaching toward the headboard, claws lightly grazing the duvet. I could smell hints of Mom's shampoo, maybe a bit of Dad's soap. Comforting. Familiar. Forbidden.

And yet, here I was. A rebel. A legend. A cat that climbed a house to touch a dream.

I tried to doze—but I had more exploring to do. I hopped down (quietly, of course) and moved out the door.

I heard Mom coming. She paused, looked at me, and didn't say a word.

Just shook her head and smiled.

As I melted into the sunbeam like a pat of butter on toast, fully immersed in my new life of indoor elegance, I heard it—that dreaded, telltale phrase.

Dad said something to Mom about "leaving soon" and "getting the keys to the car."

I froze.

My ears flicked. My tail twitched.

I *knew* what that meant. The dream was coming to an end. I was not about to be left home alone, unsupervised, free to explore closets and countertops and—let's be honest—possibly knock over a plant or two. Not yet. Not this time.

I've been around long enough to know the signs: the zipping of bags, the jangling of keys, the change in tone. The humans get that "hustle" energy. And it never ends well for me. I watched Mom glance at me with that look. The one that says, "He's coming back out."

No words. Just that slow, regretful head tilt. I

sighed.

Not dramatically, mind you—just a quiet, knowing exhale. My time inside had been glorious. Triumphant. Historic, even. I had climbed a house, orchestrated a squirrel alliance, and claimed the bed and the sunbeam. I had *lived* the dream.

And now... well, even legends must return to their thrones.

So when Mom gently walked over and reached for me again, I didn't wriggle. I didn't squirm. I just looked at her with wise, patient eyes.

She scooped me up, carried me down the stairs, and out to the lanai.

Back to my chaise. My domain.

And as she set me down and whispered, "You're crafty, Cooper," I just blinked slowly, tail curled around me like a question mark.

Because yes, I *am* Cooper the Crafty Cat.

And something tells me... this isn't the last time I find my way in.

.✍🐾

Meow Out 🐾

Cooper

Chapter 22: The Great Collar Caper

I've already let you in on my genius-level trickery when it comes to collars. Ah, yes, my very first masterpiece: The Great Collar Escape. I was purring with pride the day I perfected it—me, a fluffy Houdini with whiskers! Honestly, they never saw it coming.

After I cracked the collar code, I strutted around like the king of clever cats, which, let's be honest, I am. The humans would clip it on, all proud of themselves, like, *"There, now he's safe!"* And I'd give them a polite nod, wait precisely 4.7 minutes, and then... *poof*—gone. Collar on the floor, me on the windowsill, looking like an innocent cloud of fur with absolutely *no idea* how that happened.

They tried all kinds—breakaway, non-breakaway, ones with little bells (ugh, rude), even one with *sparkles*. Sparkles! I ask you, what self-respecting feline wears *sparkles*?

I really thought they had given up on trying to fasten one on me. I had heard Dad say to Mom, "Maybe he's just not a collar cat," as if I were some kind of wild mystery beast. (Which, of course, I am. But still—*their* mystery beast.)

But, alas, I was wrong. Oh, so wrong. I had been basking in my victory, tail held high like a velvet flag of freedom, when the clouds of betrayal began to roll in.

One morning, while pretending to nap on the sunniest patch of rug next to the door (strategically located within earshot of the kitchen), I heard it. A conversation—no, a *plot*—between Mom and Dad.

"I found one with GPS," Mom said, her voice all casual like she was talking about the weather, not cat imprisonment.

GPS.

Three letters.

One sneaky little acronym.

I squinted one eye open. GPS? Was that a new kind of crunchy treat? Or maybe a high-pitched vacuum? Or worse... another vet-related horror?

I stretched dramatically, rolled over with my tail flicking just so, and filed the letters away in my steel-trap kitty brain. If this GPS thing was coming for me, I needed intel. And fast.

Naturally, I turned to the wisest creature I know: Carol the Heron. Carol, with her long legs, sharp eyes, and that disapproving librarian glare.

So, I meandered down to the glorified pond, through the tall grass that smells like adventure and allergies, until I reached the edge of the water.

Carol was there, perched on one leg like some sort of yoga master, eyeing a frog with judgment only birds can deliver.

“Carol,” I meowed, trying to sound casual and not desperate. “What’s GPS?”

She didn’t turn her head. Didn’t blink. Just said, in that slow, feather-fluffed tone of hers, “It’s how the humans *track* things. Like migrating birds. Or delivery trucks. Or you, if they’re tired of you vanishing like a puff of fur in the night.”

Track.

Track me?

Excuse me?! I’m a creature of mystery! Of shadows and silence! A whisper on the wind! A blur of fluff with ninja-level stealth! I cannot be *tracked!*

I thanked Carol with a polite tail wave and sprinted home, ideas swirling in my brain like a pile of leaves in a windstorm. If the humans wanted to slap a GPS collar on me, they were declaring war. A *sparkly, tech-enabled, fur-choking* war.

So now, dear reader, the game is afoot. But this time, it’s high-tech. This time, I have to outwit *satellites*.

Do I have a plan?

Of course not. But I *do* have claws, curiosity, and crinkly toys. And that, my friend, is a very good place to start.

Now, curiosity is a dangerous thing in cats. It has a reputation; you know, the whole "killed the cat" business. But that’s just propaganda. The truth is, curiosity made the cat *smarter, faster,* and in my case, an unstoppable feline genius.

So yes, I was curious. Not scared. Not panicked. Just... *strategic*. If my mom was going to try this “GPS collar” nonsense, I needed to see it up close. Study it. Learn its weaknesses. All great escape artists must first know their cage before they bust it open in a blaze of glory.

So I did the unthinkable: I *let* her put it on me.

Oh, the drama. I flopped on the rug like I'd just been emotionally betrayed by a beloved chew toy. I blinked slowly, staring into her eyes, silently screaming, *Et tu, Mother?*

And the collar? Don't even get me started.

It was bulky—like someone strapped a shoebox to my neck. Heavy, as if it were lined with pebbles and guilt. And the color? A tragic shade of fluorescent blue that clashed horrifically with my soft, artfully striped fur. I looked like a rejected mascot for an outer space delivery service. I gave Dad my best *you'll-pay-for-this-in-scratch-marks on the screen* look.

"They stared, all admiration, as if I'd been outfitted by a tech startup.

'He looks great!' Mom cooed.

'Very sporty,' Dad agreed.

Sporty. Right. I'm not a runner. I'm an icon. Sleek, enigmatic, wrapped in fluff. Yet here I was, draped in indignity, the true casualty of their well-meaning enthusiasm.

But I played it cool.

I sauntered off like I didn't care, even though each step was a dramatic stomp. The collar shifted slightly with every move, as if to remind me, *Hey, I'm still here! Watching you!*

Fine. Let it watch. Let it beep, or blink, or send secret messages to satellites in space. I was going to study this ridiculous device like a cat scientist. I would observe how it worked, test its limits, and then... I would *defeat* it. Maybe not today. Maybe not tomorrow. But soon.

Later that night, as the humans dozed off (they snore like unplugged vacuum cleaners), I crept to my secret lair under the couch. With a single paw, I batted at the collar. It made a little *click*. Interesting. I rolled onto my back, stuck my feet in the air, and twisted like a contortionist in a hairball commercial.

It wasn't budging.

This was going to take more than finesse. It was going to take cunning. Stealth. Maybe even—dare I say it—Carol the Heron's advice.

I needed a plan. And a snack. Probably two snacks. Tuna, preferably.

Because the Great Collar Caper had officially begun.

The next morning dawned far too early for my liking. I was mid-dream—chasing a wind-up mouse across a golden field of shredded rotisserie chicken—when the sound of clinking mugs and human voices snapped me awake.

I yawned extravagantly, flopped onto my side in protest, and then remembered: *The Collar*.

Still there. Still hideous. Still hugging my neck like a clingy scarf I didn't ask for.

I stretched, arched my back in an Oscar-worthy display of morning drama, and slinked toward the kitchen, keeping to the shadows like a panther in a bathrobe. I perched beneath the table, tail flicking silently, eavesdropping on the unsuspecting humans.

They were drinking coffee and looking at that glowing rectangle they call a "tablet"—which, for the record, is *not* for sitting on, no matter how many times I've tried.

"There's a map," Mom said, tapping the screen. "Look, he goes behind Dennis' bushes, then across the street into the woods ..."

"Yup," Dad added, zooming in like he was spying on international spies. "And he definitely hangs out by the creek. See this loop? He goes there almost every afternoon."

I froze.

The creek?! My secret, magical thinking spot with the mossy rock that smells like adventure and wet worms? That was *my* place! *Private!* Off-limits to anyone who doesn't have whiskers and a philosophical side!

And Dennis's bushes! That's where the butterflies hang out, and the ground is soft and deliciously diggable. Sometimes I roll there just to feel fancy.

They were plotting. Decoding my sacred wanderings. Turning my majestic neighborhood patrol into a series of little blue dots on a map. I felt *exposed*, like they had read my diary or walked in on me grooming my belly fluff.

They were beginning to understand me.

"He's got his favorite spots," Mom said, smiling like she'd just solved a mystery. "He's got a whole routine."

"He's got *territory*," Dad said with raised eyebrows, as if I were running a feline mafia.

I narrowed my eyes.

Routine? Territory? Routine sounds *predictable*—a word I do *not* identify with. And territory? Okay, yes, it's true I have strategic zones: The Warm Roof, The Frog Log, The Old Chimney of Solitude. But those are private, thank you very much. Not data points for parental amusement.

I slinked away before they noticed me under the table, my tail twitching with equal parts irritation and awe. I had to admit, this GPS thing was clever. Too clever. It had betrayed me, broadcast my wanderings, spilled all my secrets like a talkative squirrel after three espressos.

But all was not lost.

I still had the element of surprise. And the ability to disappear under exactly 3.2 seconds flat. And a backup plan that may or may not involve rolling in something suspicious so they'd *have* to remove the collar for a "good cleaning."

Let them think they're learning about me. Let them trace my steps. Because soon, very soon, I will rewrite the map. With decoys. Diversions. Disguises.

If they think they know Cooper, the Cat... they have no idea what's coming.

After the GPS disaster—also known as *The Morning My Parents Read My Mind on a Map*—I knew I had to consult an expert. I needed wisdom, strategy, and a little bit of bird-brained brilliance. And so, of course, I turned to the one soul in the neighborhood who truly *got* me: Carol.

Carol the Heron.

Carol was rapidly becoming my "go-to" gal for all things confusing, mysterious, or emotionally dramatic. She was like a feathered fortune teller crossed with a grumpy librarian who had seen things. *Real* things. She didn't waste time on fluff or feelings or chasing imaginary lasers like some cats I could name (no offense to the orange tabby three doors down—actually, full offense).

Carol wasn't warm. She wasn't cuddly. But she *was* wise. Worldly—or perhaps more accurately, *birdy*. I mean, she literally flew across continents. *Continents*. I get winded just sprinting across the yard after a leaf.

So, after breakfast—by which I mean I licked some gravy off the edge of my bowl and rejected the rest like a diva—I made my way to the pond.

The air smelled like wet dirt and secrets. Dragonflies buzzed overhead, looking like overcaffeinated fairies. And there, standing statuesque and slightly judgmental on her usual rock, was Carol.

One leg up. Head tilted. Eyes as sharp as knitting needles.

She didn't greet me—Carol doesn't *do* greetings. But she shifted her weight slightly, which I took as a sign of acknowledgment. I plopped down dramatically on the bank, tail flicking, GPS collar gleaming offensively in the sunlight.

"Carol," I said, sighing just loud enough to seem mysterious. "We need to talk."

She didn't blink. Her eyes flicked once to the collar, then back to me.

"Still wearing the leash necklace, I see," she said dryly.

"Don't remind me," I groaned. "I allowed it for strategic purposes. Reconnaissance. Study. I'm building a case."

"Hm," she muttered, ruffling her feathers. "Or you've been domesticated."

I gasped. "*How dare you.* I am many things, but I am not—repeat, *not*—domesticated. I nap in sinks. I rule fences. I chase things I have no intention of catching."

Carol smirked—well, as much as a heron *can* smirk, which is mostly a slow blink and a subtle neck bob. "Then why haven't you escaped yet?"

Touché.

She had a point, of course. I pawed at the collar instinctively, feeling its solid, smug presence around my neck. This was no ordinary human nonsense. This was tech. Sophisticated. Resilient. Possibly waterproof. I had tried scratching it, twisting it, even faking a fainting spell in front of the broom closet. Nothing worked.

But Carol... Carol might know something I didn't.

"You've traveled the world," I said carefully. "You've dodged wind turbines and tangled with migratory bureaucracy. You must have seen one of these before." I just jutted my chin toward the collar.

Carol leaned in slightly, examining the device like it were a suspicious worm.

"Hmm," she said. "There's a latch on the left. It could be pressure-sensitive. Some of the humans use that for tagging birds in sanctuaries. If you apply force in just the right way—"

"With a crowbar?" I asked hopefully.

"With a *clever claw*," she corrected, shaking her beak. "Or... perhaps you find a way to *convince* the humans to remove it themselves."

Now that was interesting.

Carol stepped back onto one leg and stared out across the pond like she had already solved the riddle and was just waiting for me to catch up. She wouldn't do the work for me—oh no, Carol was not that kind of bird. But she'd plant the seed.

And that seed was growing fast in my genius cat brain.

So, I trotted home, collar bouncing with every step, head filled with plans. Maybe I'd fake a rash. Maybe I'd pretend to get stuck under the bed and meow just pitifully enough to spark concern. Or maybe... just maybe... I'd roll in something so vile, so odorous, so utterly *unacceptable* that the humans would *have* to remove the collar out of sheer desperation.

Whatever it took.

Because one thing was certain: Cooper the Crafty Cat may be curious, but he is *never* caught. Not for long. Not with Carol the Heron as his secret weapon.

That afternoon, after a well-earned nap (on Mom's chaise, naturally), I got to work.

Carol had been right. Of *course,* she had. She's practically a feathery oracle. While grooming behind my left ear—very casually, mind you, as if I weren't on the cusp of a great discovery—I felt it. A teeny, tiny bump. Slightly raised. A smidge warmer than the rest of the plastic. The latch.

It was almost insulting how small it was. Like the collar *dared* me to notice it. But I *did.* With the precision of a jewel thief and the flair of a magician, I tested it with the tip of one claw. Just a whisper of pressure... and *click*. The whole thing loosened, just a little.

My eyes widened. My tail swished dramatically. I had found the weak spot.

I spent the next hour practicing in private—curling, rolling, flopping in creative ways until I could twist my neck *just so* and reach that latch. It wasn't easy. It required the flexibility of a yogi and the stubbornness of a cat denied a second breakfast. But I was determined. And slightly offended that I hadn't figured it out sooner.

Now came the most important part of the plan: the drop.

If I were going to remove the GPS collar, I couldn't just leave it anywhere. That would be too obvious. Too... traceable. No, I had to make a statement. I had to vanish in a way that would confuse, confound, and concern my parents *just enough*—not to worry them (I'm not heartless), but to remind them that I am, above all, a mystery.

So, I scouted locations.

Option one: The hollow stump by the creek. Dramatic, sure, but it screamed *I did this on purpose.*

Option two: On top of the neighbor's roof. Tempting, but too risky.

And then it hit me. The perfect place. The ultimate decoy.

Dennis's bush.

Yes—lush, fragrant, full of dense branches and mystery. I would tuck the collar beneath the edge of a twig, just enough exposed so that when Mom pulled up the tracking map, she'd see me "stationary" in that exact spot for hours. Days, even.

She'd think: *Why hasn't he moved? Is he lounging in the bushes? Did he move in with Dennis? Has he joined their family? Have they adopted him?!*

The drama. The suspense. The *legend.*

That night, under a star-splattered sky, I made my move.

One silent, shadowy glide across the yard, across the stepping stones like a ghost in velvet slippers. I reached the bush, tucked the collar beneath the twig with a final flick of my paw, and sat for a moment in the moonlight, savoring the sweet scent of freedom—and gardenias.

Then, like a breeze, I was gone.

No collar. No beeping. No blinking blue light betraying my every pawstep.

Back home, I curled up on the back of the couch with the grace of a true escape artist. The humans wouldn't find out until morning. The map would lie. The questions would begin. And Cooper the Crafty Cat would once again be an enigma wrapped in fluff.

Carol would be proud.

And I… I was just getting started.

Stay curious, stay clever, and never let them know your next nap spot.

Meow out. 🐾

– Cooper 🐾

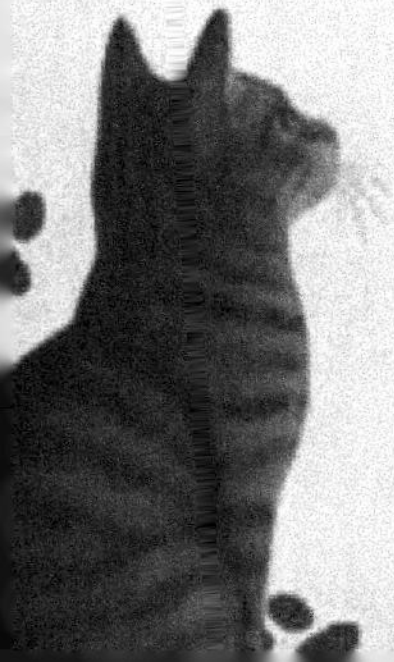

Chapter 23: While the Hoomans Were Out

Well, it happened again. Mom and Dad planned a trip.

I had heard about this for *days*. First, it was whispered conversations over coffee in the morning. Then it was murmured strategy sessions at night while they stared at glowing screens, tapping away as if orchestrating some world-class mission (spoiler alert: it was just a golf resort and a visit with *the kids* — you know, the ones who come to visit here and bring loud suitcases and leave behind crumbs and odd smells).

But then came the real betrayal:

They *mouthed* the words.

Like I wouldn't notice.

“Is *Cooper* going to be okay... with... Cheryl, the cat sitter?”

Cue dramatic music.

She’s a sweet woman, really. Soft voice, kind eyes, and a wardrobe that smells faintly of lavender and — curiously — tuna. It’s an odd combination, but not entirely unappealing. She always arrives with a giant tote bag slung over her shoulder, filled with what she calls “goodies,” which is her attempt to distract me from the gut-wrenching betrayal that is my humans' leaving. Again.

I don’t mind Cheryl exactly. She’s cheerful in that singsong way that makes my whiskers twitch. She chats constantly, narrating everything she does as if she’s the star of her own cooking show and I’m the audience of one. Worse, she talks to me like I’m a baby. A *baby*. Can you imagine? Me — a seasoned feline with street smarts, impeccable grooming habits, and a CV that includes everything from pest control to emotional support. It’s insulting... and, I’ll admit, a little endearing. I am, after all, a creature of complexity.

But Cheryl has one tragic flaw. A blind spot, if you will.
She assumes I’m **domesticated**.

Let me be perfectly clear: I am not just some housecat who naps on windowsills and plays with felt mice like a fool. I am **Cooper the Crafty Cat** — perimeter specialist, escape artist, sunbeam connoisseur, and the undisputed ruler of this domain. The backyard is my kingdom. The screened lanai? My observation deck. And Cheryl? Well... she's the substitute court jester. Harmless. Slightly clueless. But earnest in her duties.

Still, I keep one eye open when she's around. Because even a Crafty Cat knows: the moment you underestimate the cheerful ones is the moment they try to clip your claws.

And yet, when Mom and Dad leave, Cheryl tries to limit me.

No evening patrols.

No daytime walks.

"Cooper," she'll coo, "let's stay safe, okay?"

Stay safe?

I was born in a shelter with six squirmy siblings and one grumpy calico named **Beast**, who taught me the fine art of the death glare before I could even purr. My early days were filled with scrappy scuffles over the warmest patch of towel and calculated ambushes from behind litter boxes. It was there, amidst the chaos and kibble dust, that I forged my instincts. Sharp. Watchful. Unapologetically cunning.

I've stared down raccoons twice my size — one of whom had the audacity to try and steal from *my* food dish. Not on my watch. I've endured thunderstorms, vacuum cleaners, and that one terrifying week when the humans brought home a Roomba. I've rescued this household from invading lizards no fewer than fourteen times — possibly more, if you count the ones I dispatched before they made it past the threshold. I don't do it for praise. I do it because it must be done.

I'm not looking to "stay safe," Cheryl.

I'm looking to **defend the realm**.

Now, I've learned over the years that humans — bless them — are predictable. They close the lanai door and murmur solemnly, "Cooper might get out," as if I haven't already mapped the structural integrity of that screen down to the millimeter. Please. I know the exact moment of day when the sun stretches just far enough to light the weak seam above the far-left beam. I've memorized every creak, every breeze pattern, every time the latch hesitates before catching. These people act like I'm a house pet. I'm a *tactician*.

I wasn't born yesterday.

I was born with **purpose** — and claws that don't quit.

So that night, when the moon was full and the air carried the scent of jasmine and distant barbecue (Larry and Paula, three houses down, overcook everything), I made my move.

The vent in the guest bathroom had long been on my radar. It led to a crawlspace under the lanai deck, and I'd once caught a palmetto bug doing laps in there. The humans never suspected. I had clawed a small edge loose during hurricane season prep. I'd covered it with a strategically placed towel. Innocent. Devious. Effective.

Cheryl had just left. She'd sung some ridiculous song she made up on the spot about *"Mr. Cooper in his castle"* and left a *light jazz* playlist on the speaker. Honestly, what is it with humans and jazz when they feel guilty?

With the vent cover quietly popped, I slithered through with the grace of a feline trained in espionage. I landed with a soft *thump* under the lanai and paused, ears twitching, eyes adjusting.

Freedom. But also — responsibility.

I did a perimeter lap.

The frog community was out in full chorus.

Harry the Hawk was nowhere in sight, probably at some owl mixer.

Gary the Squirrel's peanut stash, cleverly buried near the hibiscus bush, had been raided (I left a single whisker behind — psychological warfare).

The stars above glittered like applause. I stretched luxuriously and let out a triumphant yawn. This was *my* domain. These were *my* grounds. Cheryl could have her snacks and feather toys. I needed *action*.

And I got it.

Around 3 a.m., I heard the sound. A low, guttural growl. Not a dog. Not raccoon. Something *new*. Something *presumptuous*.

I crept silently toward the fence line, where the shadows were thickest. And that's when I saw him.

A cat. Large. Orange. Muscular in a "used to be cute but now drinks energy drinks and yells at birds" kind of way. His collar read **"TANK."** Of course it did.

Tank was pacing back and forth along *my* fence like he paid property taxes here. He caught sight of me and paused.

"Well, well," he rumbled. "Didn't think the housecat had the guts to step outside."

I arched my back slightly, not in fear, in emphasis.

"I'm not *a* housecat," I said coolly. "I *own* this block."

Tank hiss-laughed. "I was hoping you'd say something like that."

That's when it happened — a showdown of wits and whiskers. He lunged. I ducked. We circled like fur-covered gladiators, tails twitching, claws half-drawn. But I didn't strike. I didn't need to. I let him smell it — confidence. Strategy. Sardines for lunch.

He faltered.

"Back off, Tank," I said. "There's only room for one nocturnal ninja on this street."

He blinked. Then, as if remembering a previous engagement with a full trash bin, he slinked off with a growl that said, *This isn't over*. But we both knew it was.

Let her believe what she wants.

Let them *all* believe it.

Because I'm Cooper the Crafty.

And while the humans are away... the real ruler plays.

The next morning, I returned to the house via the vent, brushed a few leaves from my fur, and took up a dignified position on the couch before Cheryl arrived.

She opened the door, humming to herself, looked over at me stretched luxuriously across the cushions, and gasped.

"Cooper! Did you sleep there all night? You didn't even touch your fish treats! What a good boy!"

I purred.

It was early evening when the front door creaked open, and I knew immediately.

Not Cheryl's breezy footsteps or lavender scent. Not a neighbor or the UPS guy with his terrifying brown monster truck. No, this was something else. This was **them.**

Mom's voice floated in like music. "Cooper? Are you here, sweet pea?"

I didn't move. Not at first.

Dad's suitcase bumped over the threshold. I heard the telltale zip of a golf bag and the distinct thump of something dropping into the laundry room (probably shoes caked with red clay — it's a thing with them).

Then came the gasp.

"Oh, there he is!"

"Look at you, buddy!"

"Did you miss us?"

"Did Cheryl take good care of you?"

That last one. That's the one that nearly made me snort out loud.

Cheryl. Cheryl took good care of me?

Please.

She meant well, bless her. She brought the snacks — tuna bites, salmon twists, the occasional suspiciously healthy grain-free chew (I buried that one behind the potted ficus). She sang ridiculous songs with my name in them. She clapped when I pawed at the puzzle feeder like it was some sort of party trick and not a desperate act of hunger. And I, dear readers, played along like a true professional.

Because that's what you do when you're **Cooper the Crafty** — master manipulator, emotional puppeteer, connoisseur of the long game.

I let her believe we were bonding. I even slow-blinked a few times. She called me her "little zen lion." Honestly, it was almost too easy.

But when the garage door finally rumbled and the humans returned, that's when I pulled out the crown jewel of my performance repertoire: **The Welcome Home Performance.**

First, I yawned. Not just any yawn — a full, slow, jaw-cracking, tongue-curling spectacle of feline serenity. Then I arched my back in a perfect stretch, one paw extended dramatically like I'd just returned from a ten-day meditation retreat in the Himalayas.

Next came the timing: precise. I wandered into the foyer just as the suitcase wheels clicked over the tile, blinked up at them with the sleepy innocence of a cat who *definitely didn't try to escape three times* in their absence, and released the softest, most heart-

melting **mrrrp** I could muster. Vulnerable. Questioning. A hint of betrayal with a generous undercurrent of "Did you miss me?"

They melted. As expected.

I circled their ankles, rubbing just enough to deposit a light dusting of fur — a mark of ownership. Then, with great ceremony, I flopped on my side, one paw delicately lifted in the air, and offered my belly.

Was it a trap? Always.

Did they fall for it? Without hesitation.

And that, my dear readers, is why I'm not just a pet.

Mom dropped her purse.

Dad bent down and scratched behind my ears.

"Oh, he missed us! He really missed us!"

"He looks so good! So calm!"

"Cheryl did a fantastic job."

I purred.

Let them believe it. Let them believe I napped all day and chased nothing more threatening than a feather wand. Let them believe I didn't knock out the security camera, outwit the sitter, escape the lanai, defend the backyard from Tank the Orange Brute, and still find time for existential sunbathing.

Let them believe.

Because that's the beauty of being me — Cooper the Crafty Cat. I rule the house *and* the narrative.

And as they unpacked their bags and settled back into the rhythm of our home, I jumped onto Mom's lap, curled into a perfect cinnamon roll, and sighed like the most contented, innocent creature on Earth.

Mission complete.

Fade to purr.

Meow Out

Chapter 24: Final Meow

Mom and Jesse wanted me to write this book because they believe I am *crafty*. I am not entirely sure what that word means to them. To me, it sounds like something involving glue sticks and glitter—or maybe something shady involving a trench coat and a fake mustache. Either way, I'm intrigued.

Let's be real. If 'crafty' means slipping into rooms labeled 'off-limits' without making a sound, then fine—call me crafty. I wear it like a badge.

You leave a door cracked open a mere quarter inch, and I can weasel in like a foggy breeze on a cold night. No one is better at finding the one sunbeam on the entire lanai and curling up in it before the humans even notice it's there.

If *crafty* means I use my superior feline intelligence to get what I want—treats, attention, a warm lap, then fine. Guilty. I've perfected the slow blink of affection, followed by the gentle paw tap and, if needed, the full-body flop with a tiny meow. I can pretend to be starving even five minutes after eating. I've convinced Jesse more than once that I hadn't been fed when, in fact, I was merely bored and wanted a little gravy snack to liven up the afternoon.

If *crafty* means I notice everything, like when Mom wears shoes instead of flip-flops (a sure sign she's going *somewhere*), or when the suitcase comes out of the closet (abandonment!), then absolutely, I'm crafty. My ears twitch at the sound of a zipper from three rooms away. My eyes track every movement with the precision of a panther on patrol.

But I wonder if *crafty* also means that I'm a little bit mysterious. Because, let's be honest: no one really knows what I'm thinking. One minute I'm curled up in a perfect cinnamon roll on the couch, and the next I'm chasing invisible creatures under the rug. I keep them guessing. I *like* keeping them guessing.

So maybe being crafty means being clever. Maybe it means being watchful, sneaky, strategic...and a little bit fabulous.

Yes. I can live with that.

I'm Cooper. I'm a cat. And apparently, I'm crafty.

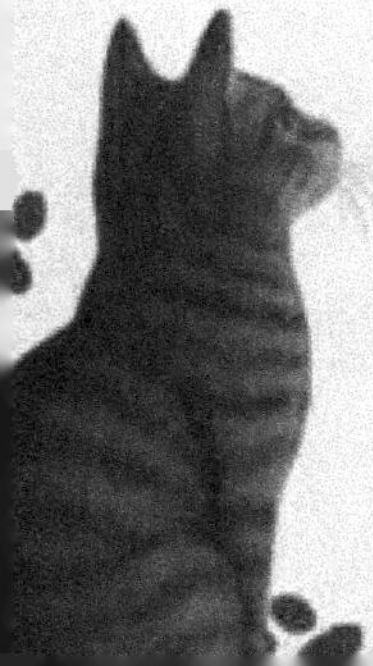

I have enjoyed sharing my *crafty* adventures with you. More than I expected to, if I'm being honest, which I usually am, unless it's about whether I've already been fed. Sitting here now, paws tucked under me in the perfect loaf formation, I've been reflecting. All this storytelling has made me realize something important:

I have a very, *very* nice life.

At first, when Mom and Jesse started talking about writing this book, I wasn't exactly thrilled. I mean, I'm a busy cat. I have naps scheduled, sunbeams to chase, windows to patrol, and the occasional rogue gecko to manage. So when they would sit near me, giggling and clacking away on that laptop, reading lines aloud with voices full of excitement, I'd mostly just yawn. Maybe I'd toss them a half-hearted meow, the kind that says, *"Yes, yes, wonderful, but could you move slightly to the left and scratch under my chin?"*

I didn't understand what the fuss was about. A book? About *me*? I already know I'm impressive. Do we need to broadcast it?

But slowly, things changed. They kept reading chapters to me. Mom would curl up beside me on the couch and read a passage about how I leapt like a ninja from the couch to the coffee table. Jesse would come into the room and say, "Cooper, the world needs to hear how you outsmarted the pet sitter." They laughed when I sauntered into a scene at just the right moment, as if on cue, tail high and eyes gleaming.

I started listening more closely. I pretended not to care, of course—classic feline behavior. But I heard every word.

And somewhere between the story about my rooftop visits and the tale of my perfectly timed hairball on the fancy rug, I started to realize... these stories matter. *I* matter. Not just because I'm crafty (though obviously I am), but because I've become part of something bigger. I'm part of a family. A quirky, loving, deeply amused-by-my-every-move kind of family.

It's funny, really. I was just a little stray once. A whiskered wanderer with no particular destination. But now? I sleep on a plush couch with a heating blanket in the winter, I get salmon-flavored treats on special occasions, and every morning, someone greets me with "Good morning, Cooper!" like I'm royalty returning from a successful voyage.

Writing this book—okay, fine, dictating it while they typed—has helped me see all the little details I used to overlook. The way Jesse leaves the blinds open just a little so I can watch the birds in the early morning light, as if he knows I like to start my day with a little live-action feathered entertainment. The way Mom always checks to make sure I'm curled up somewhere safe before she goes to bed, sometimes even whispering, *"Goodnight, buddy,"* if she spots me nestled in my favorite chair. The quiet kindness of belonging. It's in the smallest gestures—the way they warm up my blanket on cold mornings, or leave a little splash of half and half in the bowl when they think I'm not looking.

It's in how they laugh when I chase my tail like a kitten, even though, let's be honest, I'm a mature gentleman now. It's in how they talk to me like I'm another person in the room. Which, let's face it—I *am*. I bring balance, style, and a fair amount of flair to this household.

So yes, I've enjoyed sharing my crafty adventures. But even more than that, I've enjoyed remembering how many stories I've lived, how many yards I've explored, and how many hearts I've quietly won over without even trying.

From the neighbor who calls me "King Cooper" and slips me a treat now and then, to the delivery guy who always stops and waves at me when I am sprawled in the driveway, to the way Mom's friends always ask, *"How's your cat?"* before they even say hello—these tiny interactions, I realize now, are threads in the fabric of a life well lived.

And maybe that's what being *crafty* really means. Not just being clever or quick or capable of opening the vet's cabinets with my paws (which I can). But being present. Being curious. Being deeply, quietly connected to the world around me in ways that only a cat truly understands.

I'm glad Mom and Jesse saw that in me, even when I didn't see it in myself. I'm glad they believed my life was worth writing about. Turns out, they were right.

And don't worry. I have many more tales to tell. After all, every day is an adventure when you're clever, beloved, and just the right amount of mysterious.

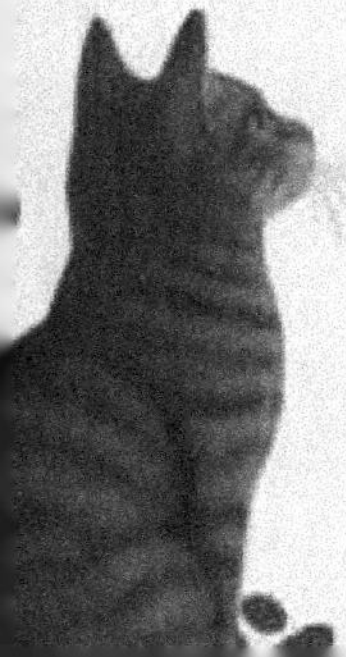

Now, if you'll excuse me, I need to go see my friend Carol.

Meow Out

Cooper the Crafty Cat:
A Tail of Wit and Whiskers

Epilogue

By Cooper's Mom

This is Cooper's Mom, signing on to verify that everything you've read in *Cooper the Crafty Cat* is, in fact, true. Yes, all of it. The dramatic tile flops, the expertly timed side-eyes, the surveillance missions from the patio chaise, and the suspiciously strategic nap rotations—every single tale has roots in reality.

I know, it sounds improbable that a cat could be this observant, clever, and—let's be honest—this full of personality. But if you've ever lived with a feline like Cooper, you understand the truth behind those whiskers. These creatures are quiet masterminds, hiding behind sleepy blinks and casual tail flicks. Cooper doesn't just nap—he strategically selects positions based on sight lines, acoustics, and dramatic impact. He doesn't simply watch birds—he conducts full reconnaissance, complete with low grumbles and narrowed eyes. And when he disappears for hours? He's not lost. He's gathering intel… or staging an operatic sulk to protest some minor inconvenience, like a missed afternoon snack.

He knows the sound of my footsteps versus my husband's. He can tell if we're packing for a weekend away or just grabbing groceries. He's figured out how to manipulate his sitting position for better squirrel visibility. And yes, he's trained us, not with words, but with an elegant combination of stare-downs, midnight yowls, and the occasional strategic paw swat.

So if you're shaking your head in disbelief, I get it. But around here, we've learned one thing for certain: Cooper isn't just a cat—he's a character. And trust me, he knows it.

What Cooper may not have told you — because let's face it, he's too busy perfecting his next dramatic monologue or practicing his tragic "no one feeds me" stare — is just how much he means to us.

Beneath the sass and swagger, behind the side-eyes that could curdle milk and the grand declarations of being "undisputed ruler of the realm," is a heart far softer than he'd ever publicly admit. There's a tenderness in him, tucked away beneath the velvet paws and clever antics, that reveals itself only when it matters most.

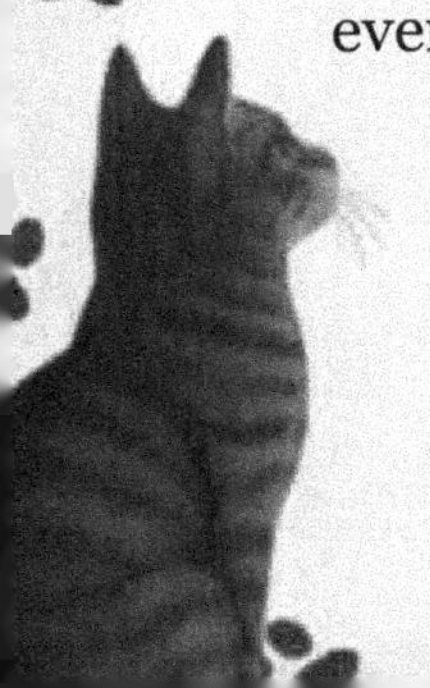

He has this uncanny sense — almost psychic — for when the energy shifts. When the air in the room grows thick with frustration or sadness. On the days when the world feels impossibly heavy, when the to-do lists tower and my patience wears thin, Cooper doesn't strut or demand attention. He doesn't perform.

He *appears.*

Silently, as if conjured by thought, he climbs into my lap with no preamble, his body curling with gentle weight, his purr low and steady like a lullaby meant only for me. No fanfare. No expectations. Just presence.

He settles in like a living, breathing weighted blanket with whiskers, pressing his forehead to my hand or resting a paw across my wrist, grounding me in a way I didn't know I needed until he's there.

He waits at the door when we've been away, perched like a sentinel with his tail neatly tucked and eyes alert. Not out of obligation, but because we are his people, and he wants us to know we were missed—even if he pretends to ignore us for the first five minutes as punishment for leaving him with the cat sitter.

Despite all his commentary—his critiques of our routines, his judgmental glances at the broom, his clear disdain for any change in furniture layout—he has a soft spot for connection. He'll saunter into the lanai where we're gathered, flop down in the center like he owns the place (he does), and stretch out with a sigh that says, *Yes, this is where I belong.* And when we laugh together or sit in quiet conversation, he watches, his eyes half-closed, purring like a soft engine of approval.

He may be a crafty cat, but at his core, he's something even rarer: a constant companion, a little soul wrapped in fur who makes our house feel like home. He's our emotional compass. Our comfort in chaos. The steady heartbeat in a room that's otherwise too loud.

So yes, his stories are true. He is a crafty cat. A clever cat. And, most of all, a loved cat. We may have adopted him.

But in every way that matters — Cooper saved us right back.

And now, if you'll excuse me, I'm being summoned by a very particular tail flick. Apparently, it's time for his evening treat—served on the left side of the bowl, not the right. Obviously.

– Cooper's (very well-trained) M

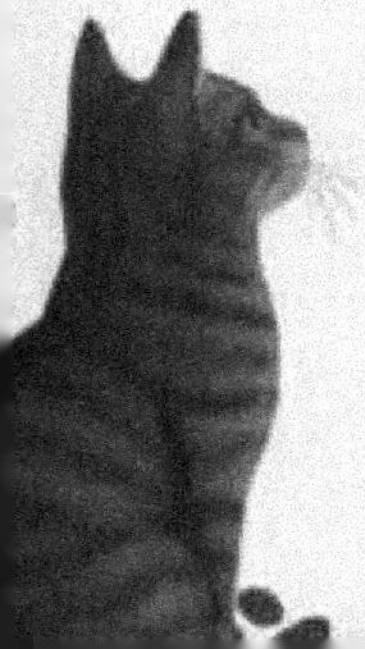

♪ *Cooper the Crafty Cat* ♪

(Verse 1)
I was chillin' in a shelter, lookin' way too fine,
Humans walked by, but none were worth my time.
Then you showed up—boom, destiny struck,
You thought you got a mouser… oh buddy, good luck.

(Chorus)
I'm Cooper the Crafty Cat, slick as can be,
Supposed to catch rats? Ha! Rats can't catch me.
I caught your whole family—yeah, that's what I'm about…
Meow Out!

(Verse 2)
I'll sneak up on shadows, I'll chase down your shoe,
I'll pee on the moles just to mark my debut.
I'd rather steal your pillow, or nap on your head,
And demand my breakfast before you're outta bed.

(Chorus)
I'm Cooper the Crafty Cat, sly as can be,
I don't chase vermin, they should be chasin' me.
You thought I'd catch critters—oh, that much is true,
But instead of the rats, I went straight for you…
Meow Out!

(Bridge)

Listen up now—rats scatter in fear,
But so do snacks when the fridge door's near.
I'm part-time pest control, full-time star,
King of this castle—let's be clear who you are.

(Final Chorus)

I'm Cooper the Crafty Cat, clever and cool,
I don't just play the game—I re-write the rule.
You thought you rescued me, but here's the big twist:
I rescued you, humans—sealed it up with a hiss...

Meow Out!

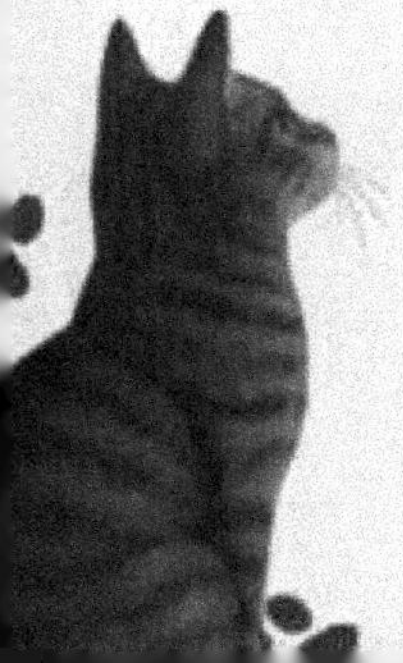

www.ingramcontent.com/pod-product-compliance
Lightning Source LLC
Chambersburg PA
CBHW081004030226
39132CB00082B/1375
9798349628061